WE LIBERALS

WE LIBERALS

By
NELSON ANTRIM CRAWFORD

Essay Index Reprint Series

BOOKS FOR LIBRARIES PRESS

FREEPORT, NEW YORK

First Published 1936
Reprinted 1968

LIBRARY OF CONGRESS CATALOG CARD NUMBER:

68-22908

PRINTED IN THE UNITED STATES OF AMERICA

TO
ETHEL MATTINGLY

CONTENTS

WE LIBERALS

A GROUP OF US sits in a room in Philadelphia. It used
to be a blacksmith shop and if it were in a more fashionable part of the city it doubtless would now be a
garage. But it is in an old, somewhat tumbledown section inhabited mostly by Negroes, and a painter and
his wife have taken the old blacksmith shop and tried
by orange and blue decorating to make it bohemian.
The painter is not a very good one. He is now trying
to follow Picasso in the latter's classical tendency.
When I first knew him he was trying, still more vainly,
to follow Cézanne, and then it was Matisse. He makes
his living drawing cartoons for a newspaper, for which
he has much contempt. (As a matter of fact, the news
stories in the paper are better than the cartoons.) His
wife is a bookkeeper who reads the *New Republic* and
Scribner's.

As I sit in the room with the young artist and his wife
and a number of other young people, I am not sure
that I belong. They are all younger than I am, and
perhaps think me an old fogy. I regularly think of
myself as young, but sometimes I awake "with a start,"
as novelists say, and realize that I am not.

Some of the young people have had a great deal to
drink and they are lolling on each other's shoulders
and telling ribald stories and making futile attempts to
sing "The Bastard King of England." The artist and

1

his wife keep recalling them to consideration of editorials in the liberal magazines. They agree in general with what the editorial writers said but dissent violently on minor points.

One of the editorials referred in passing to *Einblick in Kunst,* and compared Walden's views with those of Benedetto Croce. The leader writer is quite correct, one of the company maintains. The young painter insists, however, that the interpretation of Expressionism does not quite conform to the historic meaning of the term. Some one quotes Clive Bell. We all nod in relaxed acquiescence. Bell is a prophet of the liberal movement, so far as æsthetic theory is concerned, and liberals must follow their prophets.

There was a paragraph in one of the magazines about Bishop Manning and the talk drifts to religion. One of the young men is interested in the Black Mass. He once did newspaper work in Kansas City and there made the acquaintance of another youth who had been a student in a Roman Catholic theological seminary. This youth had endeavored to organize a congregation for the Black Mass and had himself volunteered, though apparently without diabolical authority, to act as celebrant. It had been impossible in Kansas City, however, the young reporter explains, to get enough women to participate in the religious ecstasies. Perhaps in Philadelphia, he suggests hopefully. . . .

Several give tentative assent. I gather, from the looks of bewilderment, however, that most of the company do not know what the Black Mass is. They understand vaguely that liberals are "interested in" it.

2

Eventually the crowd breaks up. It will meet again in the studio-blacksmith shop or in some other apartment, tomorrow night and the next night and every night. It will talk about the same things and reach the same non-conclusions. The painter, as I said, does not paint well, nor does he paint much. One of the other members of the group is writing a novel, so he says, in his spare time. Two or three are "interested" in the short-story. One professes knowledge of psychiatry, although he is not a physician or a psychoanalyst. Most of us work as newspaper reporters or stenographers or clerks or secretaries of this and that organization. Ask any of us, however, "What are you?" and he will never name his vocation. Instead, you will get the invariable answer:

"A liberal."

We liberals are prone to form clubs. There are frequent business meetings, at which we discuss such weighty problems as whether bills shall be paid on order of the board of directors or of an executive committee, and what new name the organization should adopt for itself in order to rally the hosts of liberalism to battle, vote, and incidentally pay membership dues in behalf of the Cause.

There are also meetings with speeches by what the program committee calls "distinguished authorities." Some of them are open forums.

On one occasion an old man arose to challenge the orator of the evening.

"My ancestors came to this country in 1654," he

3

protested. "My great-grandmother entertained George Washington in her home. I cannot hear the American Constitution, the greatest document ever struck off by the hand of mortal man—I cannot hear that inspired document slandered and a foreign system of government advocated."

The leading self-confessed liberal of the city rose to his feet.

"Pardon me for interrupting," he began, "but I do not think liberals should listen to such talk. My ancestors on my father's side came to America in the *Mayflower*. My mother's family has lived in this country since 1637. I am as thoroughgoing an American as this gentleman. I know America has stood for liberalism from the beginning, and I don't want to hear the remarks of stupid reactionaries."

A suggestion in the same club that the liberal movements in the arts might well be discussed brought a reply from the officers that "Impressionism in painting would doubtless be worthy of consideration" but that most of the members were so interested in "really important social and economic causes" as not to feel concern with the arts. Subsequently, however, apparently in courteous response to the suggestion, the president of the club made an address on modern poetry in which he ranked Alfred Noyes as the greatest living poet.

The talk at liberal clubs clings generally to a small group of subjects:

Soviet Russia.

The venality of the press.

Farm subsidies.

4

The oppression of the Afro-Americans and the question whether the club might wisely admit to membership "a few very intelligent Negroes."

The failure of Congress—always viewed with astonishment—to enact laws in conformity with liberal convictions.

Many of the frequenters of liberal clubs are the paid officers of organizations for promoting this or that liberal aim and thwarting this or that illiberal one. These organizations do not agree except in the steady conviction that "there ought to be a law," and their representatives argue bitterly. Sometimes, tired of attacking the reactionaries, they get into the magazines and newspapers with misquotations of one another, and that furnishes enough table talk for a month.

Not long ago I was in conversation with the editor of a well-known liberal journal. He was talking about the policy of his publication.

"We can't publish articles presenting views to which the editorial board is opposed," he declared. "Why, it would mix our readers all up. We liberals must uphold definite policies. Of course in our correspondence column we can print all sorts of opinions—that's a different matter."

I refrained from telling him that I had once emulated Upton Sinclair and Maxwell Bodenheim and written a letter of protest when the journal in question asserted that a liberal state would beyond doubt maintain a rigid censorship of books. Did my protest appear? It did not. Manifestly it went into the wastebasket—along with, I trust, the stamp inclosed for its return if unavailable.

Doubtless the editors felt that I was not one of "us liberals" at all, but a reactionary or immoral or an individualist or something else that contemporary liberalism in the United States of America despises, and that the proposed censorship might wisely be started on me.

The colleges and universities are often referred to as "hotbeds of subversive radical and liberal movements." I have been connected with several colleges and have visited many more. I am convinced that most college students have substantially the same ideas and views as members of the Federation of Women's Clubs or the American Manufacturers' Association. They seek nothing new, except, paradoxically, "new traditions," which they vote to put into effect at 2:30 o'clock next Tuesday afternoon.

There are, it is true, certain "liberal" groups, partly faculty, partly students. There are those who consider it "liberal" to kiss promiscuously, but whose courage goes no further; who drink with great abandon; who read Ogden Nash and in rare instances Oscar Wilde, but say they "get no thrills" from James Joyce; who write for the college literary magazine such *vers libre* as this:

> My life stretches behind me
> Many miles.
> There are days
> Grey, yellow, red, blue.

> God—
> Or Satan, if you are God—
> Make my tomorrows ripe plum purple.

The existence of this little group is always officially denied by the dean of women, the dean of men, and other such protectors of "the good name of the institution." They officially maintain that the odor of alcoholic beverages has never been smelled on the campus and in the more credulous and less sophisticated communities even assert that no young woman indulges in "smoking, reading lewd literature, or other such immoral habits."

The Y.M.C.A. and Y.W.C.A., equally reprehending the self-styled liberal group, are, surprisingly enough, more realistic. They pray for the offenders—and start "liberal" movements of their own. Under the leadership of Messrs. Sherwood Eddy and Kirby Page, they have become convinced that Jesus was a prohibitionist, a pacifist, a socialist, an internationalist, and an optimist —in addition to the characteristic "Y" theory that he was a red-blooded man and the first Rotarian in human, or divine, history. These youth gather in weekly meetings, which they open by singing "Onward, Christian Soldiers, Marching as to War," or "O King, Enthroned on High"—the latter in evident agreement with the cautious Christian Socialist who not long ago advised his followers that "there are no soviets in Heaven." They pass resolutions in favor of the New Deal, collective bargaining, honesty among politicians, and the reconciliation of evolution and Christianity.

7

A young foreign publicist remarked to me once, after he had been inveigled into addressing a Y.M.-Y.W. meeting:

"My God! They asked me, 'Do you think it would be nice for us to start a Youth Movement?' They think you can start a movement just as you do an automobile!"

There are also classes for study of "the Christian Social Order." These are characterized as "oh, so liberal and enlightening." The members of the group gather in private homes or even in fraternity houses and sit on the floor while they discuss race problems and the relationship of wages and morals. Why youthful liberals always sit on the floor, I have never discovered, although I have devoted long study and investigation to the subject. The practice is so universal, however, that when any of them are about to call upon me I know I can occupy my most comfortable armchair with perfect courtesy.

The young cynics who edit the university newspaper look on both classes of self-styled liberals with equal ribaldry. The college literary monthly never has room enough for all the *vers libre* or all the fiction about girls living their own lives, which the first group produces. The left-over copy consequently descends upon the daily for editorial features, and its rejection involves much labored conversation with the authors. In like case, are the long letters by the other group protesting against the continuance of military training in the institution and pointing out what the League of Nations should have done in Ethiopia.

The professor who examines problems candidly and tolerantly and faces facts fearlessly, whether in art, religion, economics, or science, seldom is referred to as a liberal. Parents call him "an unsafe radical," and most students, alluding to him as "a dull old boy," avoid his classes.

I know an old man who has won substantial honors in several scientific fields and who lives quietly by himself. His wife deserted him a long time ago and ran away with a sea captain. The old man talks about it without resentment or embarrassment.

"Why shouldn't she go?" he asks. "She loved him more and has had a better time with him than she'd have had with me, fooling around with diatoms and fossils and Arabic manuscripts as I do."

The old man has no canons of orthodoxy in politics or economics or natural science or art or sex. He knows the canons that other men have laid down, and he is willing for any one who chooses to live by any of them, but not to enforce them on any one else. He has lived and thought a long time, and has found most conclusions uncertain.

"I am in sympathy with every movement," he told me the other day, "simply because I believe that improvement is always possible and experiment always worth while. It is the tendency of every form to vary in any number of directions. The variations are not necessarily good or bad. The only way to find out about them is to test them by experiment. I am willing to change my ideas whenever I get a clearer view of the

9

facts—and every one else has the same right to change. If there is any absolute right, it is the right of every man to his own belief."

Whenever I talk with the old man, I think of the words of Sherwood Anderson:

"Here I am, you see, in the world. . . . I shall have to spend the whole of my life going about among people in this body of mine. Shall I crawl before them or shall I walk upright like a king? . . . Well, the devil! The question is not worth answering. I shall take life as it offers itself. For me the birds shall sing, the green spread itself over the earth in the spring, for me the cherry tree in the orchard shall bloom."

The old scholar, however, never talks about Anderson. Frederick the Great is his admiration. He has told me again and again of Frederick's edict for free speech and a free press and how the King's advisers came to him with a slanderous publication about Frederick himself and asked:

"Surely when your Majesty issued the edict, he did not mean to permit this."

"Especially this," Frederick replied.

When the old man comes to this point in the story he invariably chuckles and exclaims:

"Fancy Hitler, Mussolini, Stalin!"

We liberals, however, are not sure that the old man should be recognized as belonging to our fraternity. He did not vote at the last Presidential election, in spite of the opportunity to cast a ballot for Norman Thomas. He would like to see a number of laws repealed, and no new ones passed. He prefers the *New*

10

Yorker to the *Nation*. He reads the sermons of Bishop Cannon instead of the economic pronouncements of Scott Nearing; he says they are funnier. On one occasion, when Harold Laski was mentioned, the old man innocently inquired: "Who is he?"

It is easy to see that many charges lie against the old man, from the standpoint of us liberals. The worst of all, however, is that he has read St. Augustine and St. Thomas Aquinas in the original Latin and is not ashamed of it. He goes so far as to quote them now and then—and most of us, having devoted our study to more important subjects than ecclesiastical Latin, miss the point of his quotations. The other day he even spoke approvingly of Bertrand Russell's statement that science might sometime produce evidence of human survival after death. It may be all right for a liberal to be a Quaker or belong to some other pacifist, free-speech group, but as for spending time in theological reading, it simply isn't done. Of course, the old man is not religious; but a liberal, unless he is a Quaker, really ought to be disinterested in religion or else violently opposed to it.

The old man, obviously, is a difficult problem. If only he could be converted to orthodox liberalism! For, after all, it seems as if it ought to be possible to identify us liberals as readily as merino sheep or Ford automobiles.

OUR MASTER'S VOICE

THE FIRST THING to irk me when I became a government official some years ago was the practice of members of my staff of filling their correspondence with such expressions as "it is believed," "it is held," "it is thought." I wrote a memorandum suggesting that a more direct form of statement would doubtless be more acceptable to the recipients of the letters as well as more nearly in accord with business practice.

I had barely seated myself at my desk the next day when one of the oldest of my staff, obviously irate, burst in. A copy of my memorandum was in his hand.

"Why," he exclaimed, "we can't do anything like this." He trembled as he held the memorandum before me. "We've written letters the way we're doing for thirty years and I don't know how long before that. We can't change the traditions of years."

Fearing that the old gentleman was about to have an attack of apoplexy, I tried to mollify him. "The change that I suggested is only a minor one," I explained. "As a matter of fact, for you to say in a letter, 'I believe,' should give you much higher prestige among your correspondents than to say, 'It is believed.' "

"But I can't take any such responsibility as that." He veritably shuddered.

"Then who does the believing that you write about?" I asked.

12

He looked about him, hesitated, stammered. "Why —why—nobody. Nobody personally. It's just believed." Wherein he may have been quite correct.

The incredible linguistic caution of the government worker reaches such heights as "It is believed that the public prefer to read bulletins that they can understand" and "It is thought that trichinæ cannot survive in glandular tissue." One would think there was some ironic intention if one did not know the seriousness of the typical Civil Service employee.

Sometimes the seriousness is quite justified. A number of years ago a civilian clerk in the United States Army wrote to the magazine *Correct English* asking if *routing* were not the correct present participle of the verb *to route*. He explained that the commanding officer had threatened to fire him if he did not use the spelling *routeing*. The illiterate old fathead, with the inferiority complex characteristic of army officers, insisted that *routing*, even when the context proved its innocence, always gave a soldier the jitters, reminding him that sometime he might suffer a routing at the hands of an enemy.

The language of American government actually differs from every other linguistic phenomenon in the universe. In it every eccentricity of class and provincial dialect is raised to the highest power. The professional State Department functionary is more pompous than the Metropolitan of the Coptic Church and the Prime Minister of Albania put together. The average Congressman gives the impression of a county commissioner who has studied elocution and spelling. The

13

typical judge is a radio version of Will Rogers, David Harum, and the Hoosier Schoolmaster, with overtones of Lee Tracy and Calvin Coolidge.

Some of our early Presidents were writers of excellent prose; *e.g.*, Jefferson, Madison, the Adamses, and Tyler. Lincoln's attitude toward writing was essentially that of a poet. In later days, with ghost writers increasing in Washington as fast as rabbits on the Western plains, it has become more and more impossible to know whether a President or Cabinet officer has written his speeches and messages or even has read them before releasing them to the public. Sometimes one may draw an inference from the official's inability to pronounce the words in his addresses, but that rarely happens. Occasionally the ghost writer makes trouble, even for a President, as when some bright young man in the State Department, who knew more about European etiquette than about the American temper, wrote for Theodore Roosevelt a message extending the greetings of "me and my people" to a foreign potentate. The newspapers made a bitter attack on "the monarchical tendencies" of the President, conspicuous in the rumpus being a publication that had a rule of style providing for the invariable use of *Mr.* before the name of the publisher even when the initials also appeared.

Presidents actually are much more inclined to do their own writing than are Cabinet officers. Usually they are brighter, have less swank, and feel more responsibility. Also, they are more ready to be original. Woodrow Wilson's schoolmasterish style is unmistakable. Warren Harding's advisers and associates (who considered themselves more intelligent than he, whereas they were only less honest) flocked about to write his speeches. They produced the most laughable collection of hypocritical nonsense that ever purported to come from a high public official. It was under their guidance that he characterized American business as "an expression of God-given impulse to create, and the saviour and guardian of our happiness, and of equal opportunity for all in America." Now and then he would break away in a speech and talk extemporaneously as he had used to talk to the home folk through the Marion *Record*. Only on such occasions did his talks have any sense to them.

The gloomy Coolidge surrounded himself with aides of a dullness comparable to his, and no one could distinguish between what they wrote and what the President prepared himself. After cannily acquiring a reputation for sphinxlike silence, he produced more words, fewer of which will be remembered, than any other President who was not a consistent writer of books. The intellectual caliber of his assistants is illustrated by the oft-told story of the acquaintance of his who was unwise enough to send the President a Christmas card in French. One of his secretaries addressed the acknowledgment to Messrs. Joyeux Noël and Heureuse Année.

The writings of Mr. Hoover, the Great Engineer and Great Economist, were colorless in a different way and for a different reason. Mr. Coolidge's literary equipment consisted of New England axioms, which the public delighted to hear, getting the same pleasure of

15

recognition as when "Home Sweet Home" or "The Rosary" is sung in a concert. The good Herbert, on the other hand, knew a lot of things that the public did not, and hardly anything that the public did know.

It is credibly reported that Franklin D. Roosevelt writes his own speeches, using, naturally, data supplied by other officials and outside experts. When he entered upon his office, he had the notion that Cabinet officers and other purported specialists could prepare addresses suitable for him to deliver over the radio. The technical character of the material that was given to him, and its complete unintelligibility to the average person, soon convinced him that a President who wanted to be understood would have to rely on himself in phrasing his speeches. This he has subsequently done. In preparing his addresses, it is said, he imagines himself explaining things to individual men and women whom he has known in his home village and elsewhere.

The language of Cabinet officers varies widely with the intellect and taste of the individuals. On the one hand, there may be a "Puddler Jim" Davis, anxious not so much to give the public information about the state of the Union or even the state of labor as to convince his hearers that he and every other upstanding Moose are friends of the poor man, lovers of little children, and men whom a homeless dog will always follow once it catches sight of them. On the other hand, a man like "Call me Jim" Farley, one of the ablest prize fight executives in the United States, may be suddenly plumped into the position of Postmaster General, and

16

then, if he is to show himself an expert, must rely largely on his specialist advisers.

Of course every member of Congress who writes to a member of the Cabinet, even though he asks merely for a bulletin, expects a personal reply signed by the Secretary of the Interior, Agriculture, or whatever the case may be. He would be insulted if the bulletin were simply mailed to him. Naturally, the Cabinet member never reads the letters, unless they are of great importance. Usually he does not even look at them. He has somebody in the office trained to imitate his signature, and that serves the necessities of Congressmen and others who insist on dealing with principals. Occasionally he gets into difficulty, as when a subordinate misunderstands what he would like to say or uses language either too illiterate for his dignity or too flowery for public appreciation.

The formal publications of United States government departments represent much the same linguistic standards that are employed in university publications, although the government official shows himself even more cautious and his writing will contain not more than half as many out-and-out statements of fact as will that of the university scientist. The so-called popular bulletins, issued chiefly by the Department of Agriculture, are different. They are the result of compromise. The bulletins are written by scientists, some of whom have not even talked with a farmer for twenty years, and whose concept of an appropriate bulletin is a treatise on botany or genetics, besprinkled with Latin terms and German quotations. The farmer himself,

17

who is to read the bulletins—or try to—has, on the average, not gone beyond the eighth grade in school and knows little about botanical or genetic theory though considerable about the behavior of plants and animals. Still another factor enters in—the Congressmen, through whom most of the bulletins are distributed. There are two schools of thought among these dignitaries. One holds realistically that a bulletin should use the characteristic language of the farm. The other maintains proudly that any honest farmer, armed with a reading glass and a copy of the Holy Scriptures, can understand the most abstruse implication of the Mendelian law. The official editors are all for simplicity and tend nowadays to carry their point, albeit with qualifications. The members of Congress are, as a rule, pretty well satisfied, especially if the bulletins are long, verbosity being a cardinal political virtue. In some instances, however, they are displeased with anything the Department of Agriculture can offer to their constituents. The late Senator Robert B. Howell of Nebraska conceived the notion that the agricultural problem of the United States, or at least of Nebraska, would be solved if every farmer would plant a patch of sugar beets. He therefore asked that instead of farmers' bulletins some fifty thousand copies of a highly technical publication on sugar beet culture be distributed to the farmers of his state. The privies of rural Nebraska are still equipped with treatises on beets.

The language of the typical State executive, whether governor, superintendent of public instruction, or livestock commissioner, is a grade below that of the corresponding federal official. Few State officials have anybody available to write their speeches or even to correct them once they are written.

Some (though not much) of the matter is prepared for the purpose of being understood by the readers. At the approaches to the viaduct separating the business districts of Kansas City, Missouri, and Kansas City, Kansas, there used to be signs reading, "Minimum Speed, 30 Miles an Hour." An overwhelming proportion of Missourians and Kansans thought *minimum* meant greatest, and the traffic was slowed down to a tortoise speed. The officials of the two States took due notice and changed the signs to read, "You Must Go at Least 30 Miles an Hour over this Viaduct." Some considered *viaduct* too difficult a word for the motorists, but nobody could think of an appropriate substitute.

An amusing characteristic of State attorneys-general is their universal desire to be called by the military title of "General"; General Macdougal, *e.g.* Some of them, in calling on the telephone, instead of saying, "This is Mr. ——," or "This is the Attorney-General," say, "This is General ——." Being usually second-rate lawyers, as unlearned in the English language as in their Blackstone, they fondly imagine that *attorney* modifies *general*, as *brigadier* or *major* does in the army. A few, more canny, use the term in the hope some time of attaining a more exalted office. With a military title, they feel, they will get the votes of innumerable war veterans, who will suppose that the

19

candidates were distinguished soldiers in the service of their country.

No executive official, national or State, can equal the members of any of our legislative bodies in juggling the English language. If through a miracle the national humorous magazine, the *Congressional Record*, were alone of our literature to survive into a future age, our language, reconstructed on it as a basis, would be as strange as a Latin grammar founded on the illiterate idiosyncrasies of Julius Cæsar.

The most glaring errors, at that, do not usually get into the *Record*, because the average Congressman has a secretary of some education who corrects the proofs of the statesman's addresses and eliminates such expressions as "has went," "flaunt" (for "flout"), and "if I had of knew." Some glaring errors pass the censor, however. For instance, Senator J. Ham Lewis of Illinois, an authority on the sartorial art rather than the art of writing, is duly quoted as saying: "I speak to one known as George Norris, *whom* I delight to say is the most useful single legislator in any parliament of the English-speaking world." Likewise, Senator Nye of North Dakota, the former white hope of the liberals, announced in the armament investigation: "The chair wonders why it hadn't ought to be embarrassing to some people."

Sometimes one of the houses of Congress attempts as a whole to regulate the language of its members, as when the House of Representatives censured Tom Blanton for printing a mild oath or two (quoted from constituents) in the *Record*. What the members would say if they were confronted with a modern realistic novel, God only knows. Another row occurred when a Southern Congressman referred to Afro-Americans as "niggers." As a result, a rule of style now bars that word. On this occasion the press added to the confusion. The press associations strictly prohibit the word *nigger*. When the rumpus occurred in the House, the conscientious press association representatives took their style books literally, changed the word *nigger* to *Negro*, and quoted the fire-eating Southerner as asserting that he had always called his black friends "Negroes" and purposed to do so world without end.

The rules of style in the *Congressional Record*, by the way, are most curious. The name of any member of Congress is required to be printed in caps and small caps, even if it occurs a hundred times in a column. *God*, however, is printed merely in lower case, except for the initial letter.

When members of Congress take to the heights of *belles-lettres*, they afford even more entertainment than with their everyday language. I have no doubt that the entire contents of the McGuffey readers could be reconstructed from the *Congressional Record*. The poetry of Longfellow, Felicia Hemans, and Eddie Guest draws the special favor of the statesmen. Numerous members, however, quote from the verse of their constituents. Not a few burst into rhyme on their own account. The Hon. Tom Heflin, when he was in the Senate, used to interlard his addresses with his own poetry, declaimed with gestures that displayed to gap-

ing galleries the speaker's vast expanse of white vest.
One of the Alabaman's characteristic poems begins:

> Old Uncle Johnnie used to say,
>   You'll find, as a rule,
> In every legislature
>   At least one fool.

> Who is this man Edmondson?
>   I never heard of him;
> Is he low and stocky
>   Or is he tall and slim?

Very little of the typical language of Congressmen
gets into the United States Statutes. There are law-
yer-members and clerks and even a bill-drafting service
—to see that bills, when enacted into law, are in traditional legal form. Frequently, the laws are quite am-
biguous, however, largely because the legislators have
no idea of the meaning of words. Time after time appellate courts are reduced to deciding the probable
"intent of Congress," it being quite impossible to discover any meaning in the phrases *per se*.

The State legislatures, containing few members
bright enough even to remember a rhyme by Eddie
Guest, and seldom having adequate bill-drafting departments, fill the statute books with a mélange of laws
the language of which belongs nowhere else than in a
collection of schoolboy "howlers." For instance, in
1913 the Kansas legislature gravely enacted a statute
governing hotels, which provides that "all carpets and
equipment used in offices and sleeping rooms, including

22

walls and ceilings, must be well plastered and kept in a clean and sanitary condition at all times."

For years the automobile law of the same State contained this provision:

"Nothing in this section shall be construed as in any way preventing, obstructing, impeding, embarrassing, or in any other manner or form infringing upon the prerogative of any political chauffeur to run an automobilious band-wagon at any rate he sees fit compatible with the safety of the occupants thereof; provided, however, that not less than ten nor more than twenty ropes be allowed at all times to trail behind this vehicle when in motion, in order to permit those who have been so fortunate as to escape with their political lives an opportunity to be dragged to death; and provided further, that whenever a mangled and bleeding corpse implores for mercy, the driver of the vehicle shall, in accordance with the provisions of this bill, 'Throw out the Life-line.' "

The legislature prescribed a hundred-dollar fine for violation of this statute, which, although subsequently repealed, is still considered by Kansas politicians an outstanding literary achievement. By such critics it has often been compared to the work of Mark Twain.

The Mississippi legislature, intent always on the Negro problem, displayed its knowledge of the English language by providing that "two schools of the same color shall not be established within three miles of each other." The Michigan code, going in for language, defines more than three hundred words, ranging from *veterinarian* to *diaceltylmorphine*. Many of the

23

Eastern states took their statutes originally from England and these are full of expressions that have not been in common use since Elizabethan times. The New Jersey code, for example, prohibits crowds "routously, riotously, or tumultuously assembled."

The State legislators themselves, on the floor of their houses, combine the language of the clergy, the farm, and the barroom. The honorable members quote poetry —usually incorrectly—from the sermons of their pastors. The stories that they tell to illustrate their points are characteristic barroom anecdotes. Their everyday language, which comprises the greater part of their speeches, is that of the less prosperous and educated tillers of the soil. Sentences are rare, and when they are used the subject and predicate seldom agree.

It is an American tradition that the judiciary is sacred, even to the point of holding that not only the substance of its decisions but the language employed is divinely inspired. In colonial days this was the only safe position to take, with the King on one side and the Minister of the First Church on the other, either of them ready to clap a contumacious citizen into jail or cut his ears off. Moreover, the early judges were generally men of considerable learning, notwithstanding their prejudices. In the first days of the Republic, many of the written decisions were models of clarity, dignity, and sonorous rhetoric.

With the settlement of the frontier, however, the standards of legal verbiage, if not substantial justice, changed. There were few lawyers in the pioneer regions, and those few were distrusted. Strong evi-

24

dence of this is found in early statutes permitting a jury to be judge of the law as well as the facts. Judges of all types were elected, and their language, when preserved, is still a delight to the historian.

For example, the Hon. Hezekiah Rogers, a flower of the Louisiana judiciary, gave this instruction:

"The jury will take notice that this court is well acquainted with the nature of the case. When this court first started in the world, it followed the business of overseeing, and if there is a business which this court understands, it's horses, mules, and niggers; though this court never overseed in its life for less than eight hundred dollars. And this court in horse-racing was always naturally gifted; and this court in running a quarter race where the horses was turned could always turn a horse so as to gain fifteen feet in a race, and on a certain occasion it was one of the conditions of the race that 'Kiah Rogers shouldn't turn nary of the horses."

In contrast, of course, stood the words of judges of the federal courts and the appellate courts of the more enlightened States. The distinction still exists, though there are no longer any State boundaries for judicial intelligence or judicial nonsense. The opinions of such men as the late Justices Taft and Holmes and Justices Hughes, Brandeis, and Cardozo are read with respect for language as well as for legal learning. There is also a group of judges—mostly federal—who have departed from traditional verbiage but who write forceful and interesting modern English. Judge John Munro Woolsey, whose experience comprises not only

25

a long legal practice but the associate editorship of a French law review, is perhaps the most conspicuous of the number. His critical discussion of Joyce's *Ulysses*, in the case brought to restrain publication of the book in this country, would not have been unsuited to a literary magazine. In a more recent suit, over the ownership of the Betty Boop idea, his Honor described the famous cartoon figure thus:

"The character which was depicted combined in appearance the childish with the sophisticated . . . a round baby face with big eyes and a nose like a button . . . framed in a somewhat careful coiffure . . . with a body of which perhaps the most noticeable characteristic is the most self-confident little bust imaginable."

There are not many Judge Woolseys, unfortunately, and the current tendency, even among members of the bar, is to regard the bench as only a little more dignified than a vaudeville stage. A friend of mine, a really learned judge, recently made his first judicial circuit through a Southern state. A lawyer acquaintance approached him and said:

"You will pardon me, Judge, but I know you are new to the South, and I hope you won't object if I tell you something about our customs. Some colored lawyers will undoubtedly appear in your court. Now, down here the judge never addresses them as 'Mr.'—he calls them James, or Arthur, or Washington, or whatever their first name happens to be."

"But," my friend expostulated, "I don't know these men, and I probably will forget their first names. What

26

shall I do if a Negro lawyer addresses the court, and I don't know his given name?"

"Well, in that case," was the reply, "simply call him 'Judge.'"

Many an elected judge devotes his major efforts to convincing the electorate that he is either entertaining or profound. Hence he may spend weeks upon his decision in a case. In many instances within my experience, the time is expended largely upon verbiage—which perhaps accounts for the fact that the average appellate court is always months, if not years, behind in its work.

Most judges, possessed of some training in grammar and rhetoric, avoid arrant solecisms. Not always, however. Judge Harrington, of the city court of Metter, Georgia, recently handed down this masterpiece:

"I rule that fishing is not bad, that a man has not got a bad character that fishes."

Whenever a lawyer, in his petition or his argument, tries to act smart, the court endeavors to go him one better. In Guymon, Oklahoma, a couple of attorneys wrote a divorce petition all in bad verse, concluding thus:

"Wherefore, the plaintiff now humbly prays
 For a divorce, that all her coming days
 May be lived from defendent free from fear,
 And for such other relief as to this court is clear."

The Hon. E. Hiner Dale, judge of the district court, was nowise nonplussed. After hearing the testimony, he hied himself to his chambers and his rhyming dic-

27

tionary and after meditative study produced a decision written in verse. The judge outdid the lawyers, using not only a different metrical scheme (based doubtless on his boyhood memory of "The Assyrian came down like a wolf on the fold"), but showing himself less the limping amateur—as may be seen from the final words of his judgment:

"Wherefore it is ordered, adjudged, and decreed,
From her bonds of matrimony this plaintiff is freed.
A divorce is granted, but the costs she must pay,
The same to become final six months from today."

Verse, original or quoted, is a favorite medium of the judiciary. The Hon. George H. Ethridge, justice of the supreme court of Mississippi, author of a volume entitled *Essays and Poems*, makes this pronouncement:

"When of 'dough' we get a batch,
The women make us toe and scratch,
And he who courts and does not wed,
She will pull his leg in court instead."

When Justice Silas M. Weaver was on the Iowa supreme bench, he declared that a lawyer "is not required to forego all the embellishments of oratory, or to leave uncultivated the fertile field of fancy. It is his time-honored privilege to—

" 'Drown the stage in tears,
Make mad the guilty and appall the free,
Confound the ignorant, and amaze, indeed,
The very faculties of eyes and ears.' "

The Hon. Gus Thomas, of the Kentucky court of appeals, illustrated the facetious humor of the bench in his decision in the case of Cornett et al., vs. Horn et al.:

"The Horns and the Cornetts, who were members of the same family, became discordant. To restore their former harmony, they applied to the Perry circuit court, before which they chanted their troubles, and it adjudged them jointly blamable therefore, and this appeal by the latter brings the case here, that we might play our part in bringing the members of the family orchestra in (*sic*) accord."

It is perhaps worthy of attention that the distinguished judge is a prominent Elk; presumably he cultivated his humor in the lodge room.

If a judge cannot sufficiently entertain his constituents through his own efforts, he often calls a movie actress, an officer of the Tall Cedars of Lebanon, or some other distinguished American, to sit on the bench with him and make merry. For instance, Leon Goslin, baseball umpire, popularly called "the Goose," was invited by his Honor to sit on the Philadelphia municipal court bench. There he was addressed by the judge as "Umps," and upon being asked for advice on pending cases used the language of the diamond, such as "He's out" and "Walk him." The incident furnished copy for a full newspaper column.

If a judge has acquired a reputation for profundity through using words that the voters cannot understand, he must keep up this standing, as witness the Hon. Thomas A. Sherwood, of the Missouri supreme court, talking about a penitentiary sentence for stealing harness:

"Bill Burdette had formerly been a resident of Kansas, and while there placed a *pretium affectionis* on a set of harness; and in consequence of its informal appropriation, he was for a time forcibly secluded from ordinary social intercourse. On his release he returned to Missouri. But Charley May had also resided in Kansas and was in this respect his peer, and could thus add the *similiter* to Bill Burdette's unconventional method of acquiring property."

In a case involving a rumpus in a Greek church, the learned Justice James F. Minturn, of the New Jersey supreme court, remarked:

"The irate prosecutor apparently was imbued with the complacent and soul-satisfying notion that the ægis of American liberty carried with it, as a necessary appendage, the inestimable and consoling right of intruding himself into a body of worshipers and there publicly excoriating the officiating pastor, in language so sulphuric and esoteric that lexicographers refuse to recognize it and Holy Writ expressly denounces it."

It is in defining and explaining words, indeed, that the typical judge reaches his height of scholarship. Georgia, in common with most Southern states, has a statute prohibiting obscene and vulgar language in the presence of a woman, and at least one court has characterized such laws as equal in importance to the preservation of life, liberty, and the pursuit of happiness. Innumerable decisions define the terms of the enactment. The supreme court of Georgia pronounced that "if a man ask a female in her presence, without provocation, to 'go to bed with him,' he is guilty of using obscene and vulgar language in the presence of a female." The same court held that "You are a God-damn low-down son of a bitch" is not obscene and vulgar language. A somewhat more technical case arose when a certain Rev. Mr. Holcombe, a revivalist, remarked in his tabernacle, "You woman with the big fat rump pointed towards me, get out of the way." The Georgia supreme court ruled that this was vulgar and obscene when spoken in a church, but pointed out that the reverend gentleman could have used the words in a brothel without coming under the penalties of the statute.

The Alabama supreme court declined to rule on whether it was insulting or obscene—insult rather than vulgarity is forbidden in the Alabama statute—to say to a girl, "If you will let me kiss you, I will buy you a pretty ring." The question, it stated, was one to be decided by a jury, not a judge.

The same court was less cautious in a decision as to dogs. It ruled that a dog is not property and therefore cannot be the subject of larceny. The Maine supreme court, even more philological, handed down the pronouncement that a dog is not a domestic animal.

The general run of judges are somewhat chary of literary criticism, but indulge occasionally. The Hon. Edward J. Murphy, of the circuit court of Detroit, offered this *obiter dictum* on Mr. Guest, the heretofore mentioned author of that superfluous prayer, "Lord, keep me from the sin of being smart":

"What a mission and what a power to bring daily to millions of folk a song of solace, a lyric of laughter, a canticle of inspiration!"

The judge's kindly intention was not too favorably received by disciples of Detroit's poet laureate. They pointed out that he used "folk," not "folks" as the poet did, and intimated that he was high-hatting both the public and Mr. Guest. The reaction to this was never tested, for the good judge died before his term expired. Since then, to the best of my knowledge, no Michigan judge has ventured a pronouncement upon literature.

THE MUSE AFIELD

ONE DAY RECENTLY, as I walked through the "pea-cock alley" of a Middle Western hotel, I was struck by the absence of voluptuous women and the presence of framed sections of green burlap, on which were mounted printed and typewritten sheets. One of the sections attracted me by the extraordinary combination of colors in its printed matter, and I paused to examine it. At the top was a pink desk blotter, bearing the words:

> "When you have the stomach ache
> Chiropractic you should take;
> When you start to cough like—well,
> With chiropractic you'll feel swell,
> Of all good things that God has blest,
> Chiropractic tops the rest."

Beneath this touching poem was the picture of a young woman, whose posture and attire, despite the religious tone of the verse, seemed anything but ecclesiastical, and above whom towered a manly youth, strongly resembling a stevedore or a truck driver, in a surgeon's gown. Evidently he was the chiropractor blest of God.

As I paused in contemplation, I felt a hand on my shoulder. I turned just as a middle-aged man in an old-time Prince Albert coat addressed me.

33

"You look like you were interested in literature, Brother."

"Somewhat," I answered in as dubious a tone as I could muster.

"I just thought you were when I saw you stopping at this exhibit," the man went on. "Do you know, I wrote all these poems on this section? They're not signed, but that's because I've sold 'em to lots of chiropractic doctors and they want to put their own names down. It helps a professional man, you know, if folks think he's literary. Especially women. And I don't mind these doctors putting their names down after my poems. I've got money for them, you see. Not that money's everything. It ain't, you know. I mean it isn't. But I just don't seem to feel I have to be so careful about my grammar when I'm with other folks that's interested in literature, like you are.

"But, anyhow, as I was a-saying, money's not everything. I like to do some good with my writing, like Doctor Sheldon and Lloyd Douglas. Not that I ever expect to do the good that they've done. I'm just a plain everyday plug, though the editor of our town newspaper says to me the other day, 'Bill, I've heard lots of ladies say they turn to your poems first thing in the paper. I guess they find 'em inspiring.' 'Inspiring'—that's the very word he used. And, I tell you, Brother, it makes a fellow puff out his chest a little when he's told that by a man that knows literature, like an editor."

"Is there a chiropractic convention in the hotel?" I asked, for want of something more sensible to say.

34

"Oh, no," he replied. "Don't you know? Why, the State Authors' Society is meeting here today. These are exhibits of their work. Gosh, some of them are grand. There's Mrs. Sutton, she's written a poem a week for the newspaper in her town for forty years. And Doc Ayscore—he's down at the Agricultural College—he's published over a hundred papers on hog diseases. And Clara Terrill—why, you know, there isn't hardly a woman's club in this whole State that hasn't used some of her dramatic poems. She's going to read one of them herself tonight at the banquet—'The Orphan, the Gypsy, and the Millionaire.' She does it with gestures and everything. And both senators and every representative in the State but one belong to the society. Congressman Barnsby is going to talk tonight, right after Clara Terrill's reading, on 'The Writings of the Late Calvin Coolidge.' I'd hate to tackle a big subject like that, but the Congressman's a big man. He'll do it justice, all right."

"I have no doubt," I interjected warmly.

"Yes," said my acquaintance, "you bet he will. You couldn't go to the banquet, could you? We like to have literary folks there, and I can get you a ticket if you'll come."

Unfortunately, I was unable to hear Miss Terrill and Congressman Barnsby. I had an engagement in Detroit that necessitated my leaving at four o'clock in the afternoon. But I have attended similar gatherings of American Parnassians as represented in State writers' societies. These organizations offer the most naïve and florid evidence of the American desire to be

35

known as a creative artist, and, more specifically, a poet. Usually they persuade a few well-known authors to join, while the rest of the membership is made up of middle-aged clubwomen, verse-writing Congressmen, and other ornaments to the art of letters. The members meet at banquets, recite their verse, and discuss gravely such problems as "The Future of Free Verse" and "The Moral Tendencies of American Poetry." To furnish a lighter note, there are amateur plays and burlesques of the work of prominent members—which often cannot be distinguished from the genuine article. One of the most applauded numbers at one meeting that I attended was a series of tunes played on a saw by a leading member, who stood on a chair during his performance lest his audience miss the finer points of the production. At another meeting, the most vociferous enthusiasm was given to the criticism presented by a Methodist preacher upon a distinguished poet: "No red-blooded American should read his work; he wasn't good to his wife." Some of the societies, in which Rotarian spirit is conspicuous, join in singing "Ham and Eggs," "If an Authoress Smiles at You," and this ditty, addressed to the guest of honor:

> "I'm goin' to get well,
> I'm goin' to get well;
> If you can live with a face like that,
> I'm goin' to get well."

The oldest and in many respects the most up-and-coming of these organizations is the Kansas Authors' Club. The club was founded in 1904, primarily as a

Topeka poets' society, through the efforts of Dr. Henry W. Roby, an ancient bearded physician who wrote poetry on the side, State Senator George Pierson Morehouse, a statesman interested in Indian folklore, and Eugene F. Ware, whose verse, published under the pseudonym of Ironquill, had been widely read and recited throughout the Middle West. Older members of the organization still speak with reverence of Mr. Ware, though he has been dead for a number of years. Their enthusiasm is invariably centered on a patriotic dithyramb that he penned after the Battle of Manila:

> Oh, Dewey was the morning
>   Upon the first of May,
> And Dewey was the admiral
>   Down in Manila Bay,
> And Dewey were the regent's eyes,
>   Them orbs of royal blue,
> And dew we feel discouraged?
>   I do not think we dew.

I have heard this verse quoted not fewer than a hundred times, and never without the added historical item, probably inaccurate, that Ware wrote it on the menu card of a local restaurant, the inference being that this was the sure mark of careless, unfettered poetic genius.

Chiefly through the efforts of Mr. Morehouse, the club has grown in membership to a total of more than four hundred. Lest the observer wonder at that number of authors in a state celebrated more for the production of wheat than of literature, Mr. Morehouse ex-

37

plains that the society is no guild of professional writers. "Its members," he wrote some time ago, "extend through every grade of authorship—from those who have reached that enchanted ground 'among the six best sellers,' to those who write but rarely get in print; from those whose names are of national repute as regular contributors for our leading magazines and journals, to those whose humble efforts are almost unknown and unread."

Although the club is made up of eleven departments, ranging from fiction to science, more than sixty per cent of the members solemnly classify themselves as poets. The club is divided into congressional districts, in each of which there are officers, meetings, banquets, and the other paraphernalia of American organization. At the meetings original poems are read, while among the subjects discussed are "The Cultural Value of Literature in the Home," "Our Club," "The Advertising Game," "Journalistic Possibilities," "Canned Thought," "Literature in the Schools," and "Kansas Authors' Club Horoscope."

Two great controversies have enlivened the club. The first developed in 1914. A poem, "The Call of Kansas," had since 1907 been considered by most Kansans the poetic masterpiece of the State, and Esther M. Clark was universally recognized as the author. Suddenly an ex-teacher, Emma Clark Carr, appeared with the assertion that she wrote the poem and published it in the Hutchinson *Gazette* some fifteen years before. The charge produced as much of a sensation as if the leading pastor of the State had been caught bootlegging.

The Kansas Authors' Club leaped to the bench of authority. It named a committee of its members, including a justice of the State supreme court, which went into the matter, succeeded in collating a file of the Hutchinson newspaper, and found no evidence for Mrs. Carr's claim of authorship.

The other controversy came when the Hon. L. Addison Bone, gravel merchant and president of the club, insisted on removing the apostrophe after "Authors" in the name of the organization. 'The 's' is used to indicate plurality and not possession or ownership," Mr. Bone averred. "We are an association of authors composing a club. We *are it*. It is not something we *own* or *possess*, but something *we are*."

Professors and other linguistic lights in the club endeavored to convince President Bone—and the everyday members—that he was wrong. But he stood firm, and the society with him. Not for them discussions of the Old English genitive and its relation to modern English. Enough that the spirit of Kansas and its leading gravel merchant had spoken in the sublime proclamation: "We are it." Never since then has the apostrophe been used officially by the club.

The Kansas organization claims the distinction of having been first among such societies to broadcast regularly over the radio. Since January, 1929, it has presented a weekly program of original poetry by members. How the supply holds out, is somewhat of a mystery. The program is one of the most popular in Kansas. Thousands of farmers, tired after labor in the corn fields and among the prize cattle, sit entranced as

39

some lady poet intones a rhapsody on the Kansas sunset or pays a lyric tribute to the prohibitionists of 1880. When the program is over, the honest tiller of the soil feels an inspiration not unlike that induced by the discourse of the local soul-saver; he is ready to return with new strength and joy to swearing at his loud-voiced bull and his identically qualified Congressman.

Although in this as in other great enterprises Kansas calls herself a pioneer, other State authors' societies have improved upon the model. The Authors' League of Colorado, for instance, goes in not only for poetry but for cute little interviews with local authors on the way they get inspiration and do their writing. The broadcasts of this organization reached their peak when Willard Hawkins, editor of the *Author and Journalist*, Denver's chief literary glory, began to talk about his fiction and two of his characters rushed in with threats to shoot him if he continued. It was all good wholesome fun, however, and Mr. Hawkins escaped his threatened fate as readily as a character in a *True Story* program.

Some time ago the league began to wonder if people were really listening, and frankly asked the question whether the broadcasts should be continued. "The result," in the literary words of the league itself, "was rather flabbergasting even though intensely gratifying. . . . Letters came in from well down toward New Mexico to up toward Montana, and from the middle plains to well over the Rockies, all our friends rising up to cheer and ask that we continue. School executives, ranchers' wives, cow pokes, and business men are all represented." Much to the gratification of the society, even as distinguished a figure as the Hon. F. L. Smith, vice-president of the Carbonate American National Bank of Leadville, gave the programs his benediction.

Like its Kansas prototype, the Missouri Writers' Guild is a direct offspring of the muse. Lee Shippey, whose volume of poetical production almost equals that of the indefatigable Mr. Guest, was the moving spirit of its founding. For years Mr. Shippey was the unofficial laureate of Missouri, and one of his admirers proudly boasted that his poetry had "been felt by more hearts than any other Missouri writer." What is recognized as his greatest poem ends with these touching lines:

> "What a good world is the world which we live in,
> What a good life is this life which we lead!
> Weary we grow in the race which we strive in,
> But the reward is repayment, indeed!
> Long is the work-day, but sure is the guerdon
> When stars awake in the darkening dome;
> Gladly we live and toil on with the burden
>   Just to go home."

Mr. Shippey has other distinctions. According to his autobiography in an early volume of *Who's Who in America*, he was, while head proofreader on a newspaper, "blinded by wood alcohol poisoning and appointed post-humorist of the Kansas City *Star* the same day." Recovering in time from his disability, he bought the illustrious Higginsville *Jeffersonian*. It was in his career as a publisher that he cast about for new fields of honor and established the Missouri Writers' Guild. Unfortunately the guild no longer enjoys his pontifical ministrations. Having succumbed to a yearning to spread American culture *in partibus infidelium*, he became manager of the chamber of commerce of one of the Latin-American cities, to expond in mellifluous Spanish verse the intellectual and spiritual glories that await the hidalgo who turns Babbitt.

But the guild struggles on, challenging volubly all scornful critics. Indeed, it has succeeded in imbuing the entire State with the doctrine that Missouri grows the best poets in the world, or, in any event, could do so if mules were not more profitable.

Some time ago, pressed for evidence of the guild's belief that the State is full of Shelleys, Dr. I. N. Evrard, dean of Missouri Valley College, departed sufficiently from Cumberland Presbyterian contempt of the world to name the great poets of Missouri. He placed foremost George Creel, Woodrow Wilson's press agent in making the world safe for democracy.

The two great annual events for the Missouri organization are Journalism Week, held each May at the University of Missouri, and a week's autumn frolic in the Ozarks. The guild is allowed one day of Journalism Week, and the members enjoy the open-mouthed admiration of the boys and girls in the School of Journalism, most of whom expect, according to their respective tastes, to rival Robert Frost or Walt Mason. A few iconoclasts whose ambitions run toward James Joyce,

Ezra Pound, Arnold Döblin, and Gertrude Stein, sneer at the poets who appear at the meetings of the guild, but this contumely is only so much encouragement to these earnest authors in their task of uplifting the literary taste of the Show-Me State.

A different outlet for the æsthetic libido is available at the Ozark frolic, where the natives stare in astonishment and disapproval at the abbreviated swimming suits of the women and wonder at healthy-looking males who discuss the rules of prosody when they might be at the solider business of fishing for crappies and drinking white mule fresh from the still.

The literati of South Dakota are as devoted to poetry as are those of any other state. Not long ago I was privileged to be a judge of their annual contest. If I were still a university professor, I doubtless should be impressed by the reappearance of mediæval assonance in a poem from the state of wheat and lead:

> "Kind recompense to a man you've been
> Where beauty is so rare a thing."

Having encountered dust storms in South Dakota, I was dubious as to the scientific accuracy of these lines, though they may represent a triumph of emotion over the sordid realities of life:

> "Not even winds can change
> The endless hills."

Nothing else in the contest, however, impressed me quite as did "Bear Butte":

43

"You are a bachelor butte
You are a moody butte,
You are a stately butte.
Colossal, lonely butte—
Through æons, still, be calmly mute."

For those whose poetic yearnings run to national orders, there are such societies as the Verse Writers' Guild of America, the Bookmakers, and the Stardust Manuscript Club. Possibly the most conspicuous is the International Writers' League, "incorporated under the laws of Michigan, domesticated under laws of Kentucky and Tennessee." The society publishes a magazine, *The Internationalist*, which, notwithstanding the Communist tinge of its title, is really a periodical of solemn verse by God-fearing folk. It plans an anthology for every state in the Union, admission to which is conditioned upon membership in the society and the payment of fifteen dollars a page. For this contribution the budding poet receives ten copies of the volume—"the last work in bookish art"—and "an opportunity to have her poetry criticized by three leading poetry critics of America." These distinguished critics remain anonymous in the announcement. The promoter, president, and editor-in-chief of the society, H. A. L. De Aryan of Newport, Kentucky, stimulates interest in the state volumes by contests, in which the State sending in the most poems—and cash—is nominated as "the literary center of the United States," until some other State wrests the title away. The location may thus shift as frequently and rapidly as the views of a politician—and, curiously, the only name

44

that I recognize in the collections so far issued is that of the Hon. Ruth Bryan Owen. Eventually the ambitious Dr. De Aryan expects to publish an anthology for the United States and another for the entire world.

The league also owns a big tract of land in the Cumberlands, where it is seeking to establish a writers' colony called Vatennky, with lots at a hundred dollars each. With proper consideration for the financial limitations of the literary profession, the price may be paid in instalments—five dollars down and five dollars a month. "Have an estate, a soul estate, a bit of God's earth—at Vatennky, Heart o' Cumberlands," the league pleads.

In recent years, with the spread of feminism, college sororities, and contraceptive information, women in increasing numbers have turned to the production of *belles-lettres*, chiefly verse. When that great genius, Edgar A. Guest, was proposed—and later named—as poet laureate of Michigan, the female literati were alarmed. An independent group of Clubwomen appealed to Governor William Ellery Sweet of Colorado, who, as a member of the National Council of the Y.M.C.A., Phi Kappa Psi, and the Sons of the Revolution, had a natural passion for elevated writing. Likewise, he was not insensible of the women's votes. He immediately named Nellie Burget Miller, Methodist, P.E.O., and author of *Garden Year Book* and *The Living Drama*, as poet laureate of Colorado.

This pleased the ladies, although some of them intimated they would have preferred an act of the legislature, followed by a ceremonial in which the Gov-

45

ernor, the Lieutenant Governor, and the Speaker of
the House, should present Mrs. Miller with an en-
grossed copy of the act in the presence of reporters and
camera men while the Bishop of the Diocese stood by in
cope and miter to bless the proceedings. Legislative
action was subsequently attempted in several other
States, but with scant success, the members of the several legislatures appearing to lack appreciation of the
finer things of life. At least one of the statesmen
asked inelegantly, "How's this goin' to get a better
price for corn?" while several others, when the suggestion was broached, expressed the view that not a
woman, but a Congressman of literary aspirations,
would make a better poet laureate from the standpoint
of the party organization.

The difficulties that ensued discouraged the literary
lights, but only temporarily. Anita Browne of New
York City came forward with a suggestion: Why waste
time on the politicians? Go to the real culture of the
nation; to wit, the General Federation of Women's
Clubs. Have each State Federation name a poet
laureate. Such a stroke of genius could not fail of
appreciation. While because of rivalry among aspir-
ing poets not every State has named a laureate, enough
have done so to do more than justify the proponent's
hopes.

In several states the poet laureate has been chosen in
a verse contest in which the entries were judged by
politicians, newspaper editors, and such distinguished
literary figures.

Likewise under the inspiration of Anita Browne, the

General Federation of Women's Clubs sponsors every spring a Poetry Week, during which hundreds of programs are given in various cities and towns. For example, in St. Petersburg, Florida, where the League of American Pen Women coöperated, the program included "Tribute to the Immortal Bard," "Orpheus with his Lute," "Selections from the Classic Bards—Milton, Keats, Whitman, Longfellow," and "Blossoms from Our Branch" (namely, poems by the local literati).

So enthusiastic over the national project was Mrs. John F. Sippel, president of the General Federation of Women's Clubs, that she was moved to publish in the announcement the following poem by Bill Maltbie, her six-year-old grandson:

> "Lighthouse in the darkness,
> Red airplane flying high.
> See the men look at the light
> Through the dark of the night."

The real significance of the airship, however, is best presented in Miss Browne's own eloquent words:

"Midnight and the hum of motors breaks the placid silence of a moonlit night. The buzzing is a beacon of sound to beckon one to explore. Looking from the window, there, in its glistening glory, cutting through the night with its silver nose, glides the *Akron*, flashing supremacy as the faint glow from its lights flickers from the cabin, as it soars far above the sky-scrapers of Manhattan. The moon is a klieg light to magnify its beauty, bringing the contour of its lines into sharp contrast with the deep blue of the night. With won-

47

der in her eyes, fair Luna looks down from her far-off
point of vantage upon this oncoming intruder in her
space . . . taking from the glory of the moon its supremacy of the air over man. A faint star, lone prowler
of the city sky—pauses in its twinkling—to inspect,
even as I, this alien roamer. But I, in contemplating,
can smile upon the *Akron*—for what unexplored regions are mine. Those regions where winds are naught,
air pockets *nil* and landing fields as great as the vast,
limitless expanse of mind—through which, in thought,
we may soar at will, in the great airways of poetry,
prose and song, beckoning, ever beckoning us on and
on. . . . Ours the joy of it! Ours, the crime not
to use.

"Who. are we to stop the forsythia from blooming?
Who are we to close the portals of the mind? Listen,
listen to its beauty—even now a message at the door
. . . take pen and on—and on—write on!

"The hum of the distant *Akron* softens as widening
space acts as a pedal on the sound. Its silver hulk
balloon-like, in its telescopic shape, blends with the
night, as it merges into the distance. The moon leans
back against the sky—the one lone star has closed its
eye."

The widely publicized activities of the American
muse and the candescent addresses of Miss Browne and
similar leaders have penetrated even the souls of American business men. Not long ago a chamber of commerce devotee of my acquaintance passed to his rest in
a Middle Western town. "He wanted me to be sure to
mention in the obituary" his widow tearfully explained

to a newspaper reporter, "that he was a member of the Literary Guild."

Further, with business not yet running in high gear, these Christian he-men are interested in the rewards of literature.

"What does a guy get for writing a book?" a clothing merchant asked me the other day.

I saw a chance to implant some respect for the literary calling, and so I quoted to him, as well as I could remember them, the reputed sums earned by Sinclair Lewis, Erich Remarque, Robert W. Chambers, and others who have managed to reap a substantial harvest from their writings.

"Lord!" he exclaimed, "that's a good racket. It wouldn't be a bad business for a boy to start out in when he was young." He paused a moment, then bethought himself of a problem. "But I wonder who does all that reading," he pondered incredulously.

WE ELECT A BISHOP

REV. FATHERS AND GENTLEMEN," began the President of the Standing Committee of the Protestant Episcopal Diocese of Wexford, rapping on the little gilt table. The fifty-odd clergy and laymen in the hotel parlor, rented for the occasion by the Hon. J. Perry Baker, leading insurance agent and principal High Churchman of the Diocese, sat up straight in their chairs and puffed their Havana perfectos, likewise the gift of the Hon. J. Perry. The clergy reflected piously on the generosity of their benefactor, who out of devotion to the Church had paid their traveling expenses to the caucus—pardon me, conference.

The little gilt table giggled as the presiding officer pounded for attention, and the venerable Rector of Scott's Corners rescued a tumbler from the corner of it. He swallowed half the contents and set the glass down between his feet.

"Rev. Fathers and Gentlemen," repeated the President of the Standing Committee.

"Dr. Farnold knows his onions," whispered the young blond clergyman beside me.

"How's that?" I asked. I am always somewhat blind to the niceties of ecclesiastical discourse.

"Calling all these priests from the country 'Father,'" my informant answered. "Most of them don't dare ask their congregations to do it, but they're tickled to death when anybody speaks to them that way. Yesterday I saw old Hibben over there walk past Assumption School three times at recess just to have the boys tip their hats and say, 'Good afternoon, Father.' Back in his own parish he hasn't even candles on the altar."

Dr. Farnold looked at us with something between a pedagogical frown and an ingratiating smile. Obviously we were interrupting his discourse.

"I am not here," he went on, "in any official capacity. I am sure you all understand that. I must preside at the council next month which is to elect a successor to our beloved late diocesan—God rest his soul." Several of the pious crossed themselves. The Rector of Scott's Corners, in the midst of another drink, hastily swallowed it, and as hastily made the sign of the cross.

Dr. Farnold continued, after an impressive pause:

"Several of the clergy and laity simply asked me to call this group together in the interest of the welfare of the Church. In particular, we were anxious to get the counsel and advice of the clergy outside the two large cities in the diocese. These men, as we all know, are doing the real work of the Church. I myself was never so happy as when I was rector at Bluff City, where our revered Father Hunter is now the priest. We can always depend on the rural clergy, as we cannot always upon our urban brethren, to uphold the Catholic faith."

Again Dr. Farnold paused, giving his audience opportunity to meditate on the case of the Rev. Arthur Whitley, Ph.D., D.D., who had lately intimated that

51

the bodily resurrection of Jesus was not an essential article of the Creed.

"Dr. Whitley ought to be deposed," muttered the Rector of Scott's Corners.

"Hear! Hear!" came from several corners of the room.

The Rector of Scott's Corners slid the tumbler under his chair and rose, as if to make a speech, but merely bowed and sat down again.

"I have hoped that we might unite on one of our brethren from the smaller centers for bishop of the diocese," said Dr. Farnold.

"Amen," exclaimed my blond neighbor, and there was an echo of "Amens" throughout the room. "Apple sauce," he commented to me. "They couldn't agree on one in a thousand years."

The Rev. Willis Wilbraham, a tall, cadaverous priest with a shock of white hair, rose slowly from the depths of an arm chair.

"Reverend Sir—Reverend Father, I should say," he began. "I have been rector of St. Paul's Church, Wilsonville, for nineteen years—twenty years next Ascension Day. I appreciate deeply what has been said about us of the rural clergy. They have borne the burden and heat of the day. But let us consider the interests of the diocese. The diocese needs a bishop of counsel and understanding, of wisdom and ghostly strength. But it needs not less than these a bishop who understands the problems of both the city and the country, and who can influence the wealthy congregations of this diocese to give to the country work the support of

52

which it is worthy. I see no reason why we should not unite enthusiastically upon our beloved President of the Standing Committee, the Rev. Dr. Farnold."

There was a burst of handclapping. Dr. Farnold half rose from his chair by the gilt table and made a vague gesture of dissent. "I am only a humble priest," he said in a low voice.

The Rev. Hamilton Arkwright, diocesan superior of the Confraternity of the Blessed Sacrament and the Guild of All Souls, got up, fingering the crucifix on his watch chain.

"What the Church needs is humble priests," he proclaimed. "No man need apologize for being a humble priest. Many of you think of me as a ritualist. I am frank to say that originally I thought of a priest like Father Williams, of the Order of St. John the Evangelist, for bishop. But this is not a diocese that would elect Father Williams. We all—at least all of us here, priests and laymen who believe in the faith—can agree on Father Farnold. We who are true to the Church need to unite our forces against heresy and schism. I move that it be the sense of this gathering that Father Farnold is the most eminently qualified priest available for the bishopric. Are there any remarks?"

There were none. Some of the gathering were becoming fidgety, for the hour was at hand when cars were to be at the hotel to carry the group to the Country Club, to be guests of the Hon. J. Perry Baker at "a stag dinner with entertainment." The motion was carried unanimously. Dr. Farnold, noting the anxiety of some to depart, merely rose and said:

53

"Rev. Fathers and Gentlemen, I humbly thank you."

A week later the Low Churchmen held a similar gathering in the other principal city of the diocese, with the Hon. George King Whitnam, banker and wholesale grocer, as paying host. It was admitted that the High Churchmen had stolen a march on the Evangelicals, but it was felt that Mr. Whitnam's resources in food, drink, and entertainment might overcome the effect of this. The country clergy, however—though many of them, sensing an opportunity for a good time, attended the meeting—felt bound by their vote for Father Arkwright's motion. Finally, the caucus was wrecked by a dispute over alcohol. As in most Episcopalian gatherings, there were a few prohibitionists, and these expressed themselves as deeply shocked over the serving of beer. They would never support any one "who used liquor to win votes"! On the other hand, the "wets" insisted that Banker Whitnam could afford champagne and had no contempt deep enough for a man "cheap enough to offer merely beer to gentlemen."

The result was the election of Dr. Farnold on the first ballot when the council met the following month. He still lives, a successful bishop, placating the wets and the drys, the New Dealers and the rugged individualists, the Catholics and the Evangelicals, the conservatives and the liberals. Best of all, he, like St. Paul, "suffers fools gladly."

When it becomes known in a diocese that a bishop is to be elected, either because of the death of the diocesan or because of his request for a coadjutor or a suffragan, there is immediate activity on the part of the ecclesiastical politicians. To be perfectly truthful, these gentlemen often get wind of the situation before any public announcement. They know that the bishop is about to die, or they learn in advance of his desire for an assistant. This gives them an advantage comparable to that of a stock market operator who gets the tip that Harrison Radium is going to pay a dividend two months hence for the first time in four years.

Bishops in the P. E. Church, as it is called by Southern Evangelicals nourished on M. E., M. P., U. B., and other ecclesiastical abbreviations, or the PECUSA (a typically British abbreviation of Protestant Episcopal Church in the United States of America), as it is termed, satirically, by Anglo-Catholics anxious to change its name, are elected in a manner known nowhere else in Christendom. In a diocese the council, or convention, or synod—the name varies in different dioceses—elects the bishop. This body consists of the active clergy, and delegates from the parishes and missions.

The lineup of certain elements in a diocese may be predicted in advance. There are the Catholics—or "High Churchmen," though they resent this name—as a rule made up chiefly of the clergy; the Low Churchmen, and the Broad Churchmen. The last is a small group in most dioceses. Generally speaking, the money is on the side of the Low Churchmen; contrary to popular belief, there are few wealthy High parishes. The fighting spirit is usually on the side of the High

55

Churchmen. The problem of each group is to line up enough of the moderates or neutrals or those only casually interested—mostly laymen—to get a majority. In all dioceses, the clergy and the lay delegates from parishes vote separately, and a majority of each is necessary to a choice.

In a few dioceses, the clergy vote their selection, and the laity have the power only to accept or reject. In such a case, they usually reject two or three candidates, just to teach the clergy a lesson, and then accept a candidate much inferior to the earlier choices. Whatever the method of procedure, the laity can be counted on to throw monkey wrenches into the machinery. Hopelessly ignorant of ecclesiastical matters, they have an ineradicable suspicion of any priest who is honest, quiet, and a gentleman. I know several lay delegates to a certain diocesan convention who were much disgruntled over the inadequacy of their votes to elect a certain candidate. Upon being pressed for reasons for their preference, they pointed out that their choice regularly wore a velvet waistcoat, which was their ideal of clerical elegance.

Despite the necessity of lay votes to an election, the clergy are ordinarily in greater or less control of the situation. They have little to do at home except celebrate the Holy Eucharist and say their Offices, and they can wear out the lay delegates if necessary, keeping the council in session indefinitely. When the laymen, anxious to get back to the hotel to start a quiet game, or even to return to their homes and await a future council, seek to adjourn, some priest will rise.

"Vote by orders, Reverend Chairman," he will demand. Whereupon the vote of the clergy and the laity on the motion to adjourn must be taken separately—and the council usually does not adjourn. In the Diocese of Fond du Lac, where a Low Church clergyman is as ill at ease as a tap dancer among Shakespearean actors, the laity have never been wholly converted to the Catholic point of view. Yet, whenever a bishop is elected, an outstanding Catholic is invariably chosen. All that the laity succeed in doing is to keep out a man who would introduce rosaries and Benediction of the Blessed Sacrament into every parish.

In the election itself, all the approved American political practices are employed. Chief among them is publicity. Not a few bishops are willing to pick their successors, or their coadjutors. Unluckily, they cannot do this by appointment. A bishop can, however, give his candidate prominent places on the programs of ecclesiastical gatherings, where he will be seen by many of the faithful and read about by many others through the press releases sent out by the diocesan publicity bureau. If wise, the bishop does not give his candidates a chance to celebrate the Holy Communion in the presence of the assembled multitude. He is certain to displease through what he does or doesn't do in the course of the ceremonial. The Low Churchmen watch for genuflections and other stigmata of the Vatican. The High Churchmen spot such errors as failure to keep the thumb and first finger together during the Canon and the omission of the *Dominus vobiscum* before the *Sursum corda*. Occasionally a priest proves

57

too "High" even for most of the Catholics. One priest
of my acquaintance lost all chance of a fine bishopric
because it was reported that he consecrated on the
corporal instead of the paten. I have known the president of the Standing Committee of a diocese, himself a
candidate for bishop, wisely to decline to take charge
of the opening service of the council under the watchful
eyes of all the varieties of Churchmen present.

Publicity, of course, may be operated against as well
as for a man, as any American political campaign
shows. Pictures of the clergy in all the panoply incident upon a meeting of the Catholic Congress are
viewed by the country clergy and laity with the same
awed but pleasurable guilt with which a boy from home
examines the picture post-cards offered by the hawkers
outside the American Express office in Paris. But they
are as reluctant to elect one of the participants to the
episcopal dignity as any Iowan would be to marry one
of the girls in the *Folies Bergère*. On the other hand,
quiet circulation of some Broad Churchman's remarks
on trial marriage or some Low Churchman's praise of
the Methodists will stir the country delegates to almost
equal reprehension.

The Right Rev. William Thomas Manning, D.D.,
S.T.D., D.C.L., LL.D., *Chevalier de la Légion d'Hon-
neur*, Delta Tau Delta, was elected Bishop of New
York through the misguided publicity efforts of the
Hon. William Randolph Hearst. Dr. Manning was
none too popular in the diocese; he had been the first
rector of Trinity Parish to be refused election as dele-
gate to the General Convention. On election morning,

58

however, there were distributed to the delegates copies of an editorial by the redoubtable Hearst asking if they wanted a foreigner for bishop (Dr. Manning being a native of Northampton, England). Most of them had long had it in for the impious newspaper owner, but they never had had a fair chance to swat him. Now was their opportunity. They promptly elected Dr. Manning, sang the Doxology in behalf of the Low Churchmen and the *Te Deum* in behalf of the High Churchmen, and adjourned. Opponents of the godly doctor voted for him with joy in their hearts. Had it been possible to conduct a mediæval *auto-da-fé* with Publisher Hearst as the central figure, it would have been voted unanimously.

The influence of the rural clergy and laity, who even in a diocese like New York hold the balance of power, was strikingly shown in a previous election. The rectors of all the rich and aristocratic parishes of the city were receptive to the bishopric when the Right Rev. David Hummel Greer, growing old, asked for assistance. The row became quite acrimonious—needlessly so, as it later turned out. For when the convention met, one of the country clergy bashfully nominated the Rev. Charles Sumner Burch, a former newspaper man, who, taking orders somewhat late in life, had spent most of his subsequent career as archdeacon, visiting the little country parishes and missions. What was the astonishment of the reverend rectors of St. Bartholomew's, St. George's, St. Mary the Virgin's, and the rest, to find that all their votes together were fewer than Dr. Burch's. He was elected and eventually suc-

59

ceeded the older bishop, thereafter passing to his reward.

The circulation of scandalous stories about candidates for the episcopal office has had some vogue in the less civilized dioceses. Such tales usually concern supposed excessive drinking and interest in women. One excellent priest was defeated for the bishopric largely because it was alleged that members of a military company of which he was chaplain referred to him as "Holy Joe."

Stories are passed about in the same way as in the well-known political "whispering campaign." An ecclesiastical politician assembles his friends, including a sufficient number of loose-tongued women.

"None of us, I know, favor Dr. McDougal for bishop," he begins portentously. "But we want to be fair to him. Some people are circulating a rumor that he drinks and that he holds hands with women who call at his study. I'm sure that isn't true, and I just wanted to tell you about it so that you could deny it in case any one mentions it in your presence. Dr. McDougal is probably a good man, and we want to be fair to him."

Within a week a story will be going the rounds that he has to drink a quart of whisky in order to preach, and that he has eleven illegitimate children, four of them mulattoes.

The election of a bishop by a diocese must subsequently be approved by a majority of the bishops holding jurisdiction in the Church and by a majority of the standing committees of all the dioceses. If the

General Convention is in session, a majority vote in the House of Bishops and in the House of Deputies suffices.

Approval of elections is usually a mere formality, but occasionally it becomes a grim and forbidding gate, especially when some pious soul, convinced that the Church is in peril, decides that the guidance of the Holy Ghost is insufficient and proceeds to garner in negative votes. For example, half a century ago, the famous James De Koven was prevented from becoming a bishop by Low Churchmen fearful of his sacramental views. Though still a young man, he unluckily died before the High Churchmen had the opportunity to get a steam roller started in the opposite direction. Even so, they might not have succeeded, though they gave the Rev. Phillips Brooks some anxious moments when he was elected Bishop of Massachusetts over Father Arthur Crawshay Alliston Hall, of the Order of St. John the Evangelist, later Bishop of Vermont. Indeed, Dr. Brooks had been reduced to a state of pious resignation to the will of God before it was finally announced that the bishops and standing committees had approved his election.

The High Churchmen met another defeat in 1921, when the Rev. Herbert Shipman, the rector of the fashionable Church of the Heavenly Rest, was elected suffragan bishop of New York, and Dr. Frederic Cook Morehouse, then editor of the *Living Church*, attacked him through the columns of his magazine. Dr. Shipman was at the time a member of the board of directors of the Society for the Promotion of Evangelical Knowledge, and the *Chronicle*, the organ of the society, had been making bitter assaults on both ritualism and socialism in the Church. Dr. Morehouse asserted that Dr. Shipman was responsible and that on one count or the other he would, as bishop, be at swords' points with a majority of the parishes in the diocese. The redoubtable Milwaukee editor rallied considerable support, but not enough. A good many even of the Catholic Churchmen looked on the incident merely as a quarrel between journalists. Their view appears to have been justified, for the good doctor, attaining to the Episcopal purple, resigned his position in the famous society and until his death blessed incense at Solemn Mass with as much unction as if he had been the Pope.

In considering episcopal elections, the bishops are much less censorious than the standing committees. Well-fed, well-upholstered, and confident of the power of the apostolic succession to transform a weak brother, they usually vote almost unanimously to confirm an election. They have upset only two elections in the history of the Church. One was in the Diocese of Kansas twenty years ago, when the Low Churchmen, after an acrimonious convention, polled a majority for a well-known clergyman. It developed that the reverend gentleman had a divorced wife living. True, he had not remarried, and nobody maintained that the divorce had cast any personal discredit upon him. The Right Rev. William Croswell Doane, D.D., LL.D., D.C.L., however, despite his eighty years, jumped into the fray as if he were a youth of twenty. A divorced man for bishop? God forbid. Think of reading over him the epistle for the Consecration of a Bishop, "A Bishop then must be blameless, the husband of one wife . . . one that ruleth well his own house, having his children in subjection with all gravity; (for if a man know not how to rule his own house, how shall he take care of the church of God?)" The friends of the bishop-elect succeeded in preventing for some time the announcement of the bishop's votes, but the partisans of "no divorced bishops" held firm, and the candidate at last withdrew.

The other refusal of the reverend fathers in God to confirm an election came more recently and involved the race question. The Diocese of Arkansas gathered in convention to elect a bishop—unfortunately, as it turned out, in the parish of one of the principal nominees. A number of Negro delegates, belonging to the Afro-American Convocation of the Diocese of Arkansas, appeared, perplexing the rector not a little. They should have, he felt, a Mass separate from that of the white communicants, but where? Finally he gave them a room in the crypt—ecclesiastical language for *basement*. The condition of the room, in the opinion of the black brethren, was such as to dishonor the Blessed Sacrament, and they did not hesitate to say so. Which made a new problem for the white Churchmen, especially those with Catholic leanings; whether to stand by the traditional Arkansas view that the doings of white men are invariably pleasing to God or to resent the dishonor allegedly shown to the Almighty's presence on the altar.

The result was an unintentional compromise. The rector got enough votes to be elected bishop, but the

Negroes and their white supporters dispatched a circular letter about the affair to all members of the House of Bishops, and the latter turned the election down.

While the laity, none too familiar with the intricacies of ecclesiastical procedure, usually confine their politics to the diocesan councils, occasionally they kick up a row in the national Church. When the Rev. Frederic Ebenezer John Lloyd was elected bishop coadjutor of Oregon in 1905, a faction of the laity opposed to his election promptly wrote to him and urged him to stay in Chicago. They would be loyal to him if he became bishop, but—. The "but" meant a lot, for when Dr. Lloyd tartly declined to follow the advice of this minority, they sent a long letter to the bishops and standing committees, urging numerous objections to the bishop-elect. When it began to look as if the letter might procure enough votes to defeat his confirmation, Dr. Lloyd declined the election. The more he thought about these contumacious laymen, the madder he got, and the next year he entered the Church of Rome, where the gates of heaven may be officially closed to the recalcitrant. Unfortunately, he was married and consequently could not take Holy Orders. He finally became a member of the Illinois legislature, and, still later, joined the so-called American Catholic Church—a small body claimed by both Anglicans and Romanists to be schismatic if a Church at all—and became its archbishop and primate.

For missionary districts, bishops are elected my majority vote of the House of Bishops, and confirmed by the standing committees or by the House of Deputies of General Convention if in session. It is only in late years that any sessions of the House of Bishops are open to the public, and even now elections are in "executive session." They are actually not much more secret than the executive sessions of a legislature, but none of the ecclesiastical journals has as yet developed the courage to publish the actual votes.

The voting usually takes many ballots. In addition to the usual controversy among the Catholics, the Broad Churchmen, and the Evangelicals, the various bishops have pet clergy whom they would like to raise to the rochet—or miter—and whose claims they urge with much eloquence. Even bishops, sustained by God, grow tired. Some of them are willing to go home and break a quorum, and unfortunately the House of Bishops has no sergeant-at-arms to lock the doors and round up contumelious absentees. When a number of bishops are to be elected at one session and voting is prolonged, it is not uncommon practice to decide to confine the voting on remaining bishoprics to priests who have received votes on previous ballots but not enough to elect. Consequently, it may happen that the rector of the Church of St. James the Less, Powerville, who received three votes for Bishop of Liberia and two votes for Bishop of Hankow, is triumphantly elected to some difficult missionary field in the Far West. When a session of the House of Bishops for election purposes is held, it is not uncommon to see groups of the lower clergy standing about expectantly, like Yale boys on Tap Day.

In its elections the House of Bishops moves in quite

65

as mysterious a way as God is reputed to do. One man is chosen because he is a third cousin of a former President of the United States. Another—and this might apply to many—is a notable figure in Rotary. A third shows so much respect for the episcopal office that it ought to be conferred upon him. The present bishop of the Missionary District of Eastern Oregon refers to himself as "a high-class consecrated traveling salesman." The late bishop of North Dakota, the Right Rev. John Poyntz Tyler, was picked from a little Maryland town and until his consecration had never been west of Chicago or in a temperature below zero. A former bishop of Oklahoma came from a rich parish in Minneapolis and eventually became so weakened in health and so weary of the cowboys and Indians in his neighborhood and the High Churchmen in the District of Salina adjoining, that he resigned. The bishops of districts in foreign parts, such as Liberia and Haiti, are usually more experienced in their fields.

The High Churchmen always count on a clergyman's becoming more ritualistic once he becomes a bishop. Few men can resist even the lure of purple and fine linen; still fewer, the attraction of lace surplice, brocade cope, and cloth-of-gold miter. Occasionally, however, an error is made. When the Rev. John C. Sage was elevated to the bishopric of Salina, he inherited a Catholic service, which he promptly threw overboard. Old Low Churchmen were installed instead of the young Catholic priests that his predecessor had favored. Incense no longer perfumed the Cathedral. "Father" was a form of address in bad odor, and to speak of "saying Mass" was to court hydrophobia on the part of the bishop. The High Churchmen were mad all through—not only within the district, but outside. They soon saw their chance for a flank attack. The Cathedral had been given as a memorial on condition that Mass be celebrated daily in it forever. The bishop had abandoned the daily services. The High Churchmen would back a suit to void the bequest of the building. Whether it were successful or not, it would, they figured, finish the bishop. And so it did. In the gathering storm, the ordinary had a heart attack and conveniently passed to his reward.

Not only in Churchmanship do the bishops grow. The lowest Churchman ever elevated to the episcopate can, in a grey suit and a four-in-hand tie, exhibit greater hauteur than the most Catholic rector arrayed in a lace-trimmed alb and a fourteenth-century chasuble. The late Right Rev. Alexander Mackay-Smith, D.D., sometime the Low Church diocesan of Pennsylvania, was, the story goes, met on his return from Europe by an earnest and pious but socially unimportant female communicant. She grasped him by the hand.

"My dear Bishop Smith, I'm so delighted you are back with us again," she exclaimed.

The Bishop drew himself up to his full height. He withdrew his hand.

"Madame," he proclaimed with dignity, "I am Bishop Mackay-Smith, not Bishop Smith."

Perhaps the superhuman dignity of most bishops is a reason why many laymen really want for their diocesan "a real he-man, a fellow you can know from hell to breakfast and back," as one of them elegantly put it to me. A psychoanalyst would doubtless refer it to a desire to pat God—or their fathers—on the back. At any rate, the number of backslapping bishops is steadily growing. In the Diocese of Milwaukee, where the bishop ordinarily confines himself to such societies as the Clerical Union for the Maintenance and Defense of Catholic Principles and the Confraternity of the Blessed Sacrament, it was a comfort to the laity to obtain as a coadjutor—and subsequently as diocesan—the Right Rev. Benjamin Franklin Price Ivins, who in the late holy war was enough of a go-getter to be charged with the organization of civilian labor for the spruce division of the United States Army. Likewise, the Right Rev. John Chamberlain Ward, ordinary of Erie, served in the war, was wounded, and devotes more than a third of his space in *Who's Who in America* to recording his military services, including membership in the American Legion. Most of the right reverend fathers, before they ever got to be bishops, made sufficient concession to the lay point of view to become Masons, and some even Shriners, though only the Right Rev. William Blair Roberts, bishop of South Dakota and the Right Rev. Eugene Cecil Seaman, bishop of North Texas, publicly admit the latter fact. Most of them, of course, joined high-toned fraternities in college, and thus gained a reputation as good fellows. One of them, the Right Rev. Gouverneur Frank Mosher, bishop of the Philippines, even boasts of his membership in Theta Nu Epsilon. That he has not been translated to some wealthy diocese in the States must be due only to lack of appreciation on the part of the ignorant laity of the qualifications which membership in T. N. E. represents. In the South, Knights of Pythias often become bishops, as witness the Right Rev. Thomas Campbell Darst (also a Mason and a Pi Kappa Alpha), bishop of East Carolina, and the Right Rev. William Mercer Green, coadjutor of Mississippi. In the staid old diocese of Maine the incumbent of the bishop's throne, the Right Rev. Benjamin Brewster, S.T.D., is a life member of the Benevolent and Protective Order of Elks, and proud of the fact.

In some of the 100 per cent American states, membership in Rotary is practically a prerequisite to election to the episcopate. Not a few of the right reverend clergy boast of belonging to this order in their autobiographical sketches in *Who's Who in America*. Others refrain from advertising the fact that Thursday noons they are slapped on the back and called "Charley" or "Jim" or "Francis" by he-men, instead of having their episcopal rings kissed by beautiful women. Some of the less baronial societies of the red-blooded also have bishops in their membership. For instance, the Right Rev. Frank W. Sterrett, bishop of Bethlehem, and the Right Rev. Middleton Stuart Barnwell, ordinary of Idaho, are Kiwanians. Despite his membership in the ascetic Order of the Holy Cross and his presumable contempt for the joys of this world, the Right Rev. Robert Erskine Campbell, missionary bishop of Liberia until poor health compelled his retirement, is a Civitan.

A priest becomes a profound scholar immediately upon his elevation to the episcopate. Not only is this recognized by the press, which interviews him on every subject from the Alexandrine Codex to the influence of Communism in Estonia, but all well-regulated theological seminaries attest the fact by conferring the doctorate of divinity of sacred theology. At least one of them has a published rule that the degree shall be conferred on any alumnus or former student who is elected bishop and thus makes good for dear old *alma mater*.

Negro bishops have long been a problem. The Episcopal Church has some thousands of colored communicants, and these among the proudest and richest members of their race. Naturally, they want to have bishops, and, as naturally, their clergy want to be bishops. Nobody enjoys being a bishop more than does a Negro, and after seeing one of them celebrate Pontifical High Mass in the midst of an array of black acolytes, glittering candles, and clouds of incense, I am inclined to think nobody is better qualified.

The Episcopal Church, however, clings closely to the theory of exclusive episcopal jurisdiction; it maintains that a bishop has jurisdiction over the entire territory of his diocese—holding, for instance, that the Roman Catholic bishop is the local missionary of a foreign church, and, of course, that the Methodists, Baptists, and such folk have nothing that can be called a church at all. Consequently, a Negro diocese could not be created—and the white communicants would never stand for a Negro diocesan over even the smallest number of white folk. After much argument, a plan was devised whereby Afro-American convocations should be organized in the South and suffragan bishops attached to dioceses should be put over them. The plan was put into effect only in the Carolinas and in Arkansas, such states as Alabama and Mississippi being already too much afraid of the "evil eye" and other voodoo influences attributed to colored folk to add the apostolic succession to the Negro's powers.

A native white of that benighted region once told me of the goings-on in a colored Episcopal Church in his neighborhood.

"Yes, suh! Yes, suh!" he protested in response to my polite expressions of doubt. "They burn candles up in front and they bow down and they make funny signs on themselves. They're worshiping anti-Christ, the old devil himself." The perspiration stood out on his brow as he told his story.

In point of fact, the average colored communicant in the South knows much more theology and liturgics than his white brother. Entertaining, but not altogether palatable to Southern tastes, is the fact that the Righ Rev. Edward Thomas Demby, the colored suffragan of Arkansas, holds more academic degrees than any Southern white bishop, and more than most Northern ones. Bishop Demby holds a B.D. from Wilberforce University, an S.T.D. from the University of Chicago, a D.D. from Paul Quinn College, a Litt.D. from Selma University, a Mus. B. and an LL.D. from Oskaloosa College, and another LL.D. from Wilberforce University.

71

Certain young men are destined of God to sit on the episcopal throne. So unerringly does the Holy Ghost operate in such instances that one may classify these young men with assurance:

1. Young priests who play pinochle and cribbage with the higher clergy, smooth out rows between the bishops and influential laymen, write publicity stories on the sermons of the ordinary and the unprecedented achievements of the diocese, and act generally as "yes-men." Not infrequently such young men rejoice in the resounding title of "Chaplain to the Right Rev. the Bishop," though their chaplaincy may involve nothing more than saying grace at the bishop's table, where they customarily eat and thus save expenses. One such chaplain, however, overplayed his hand. He became involved with a young woman relative of his lordship and was unceremoniously unfrocked. The bishop was too far removed from his college athletic days to administer a salutary kick to the seat of the young man's trousers, but he was seen to throw the youth's bag down the steps of the episcopal palace as the erstwhile chaplain darted toward a taxicab. Another young man of my acquaintance is now spending all his spare time— which means about seven hours a day—instructing the bishop's family in the intricacies of contract bridge. As he has the record of a club championship in the game and is apparently as good a teacher as player, I have no doubt that the minute he becomes thirty years old— the minimum age for bishops—he will be nominated for some vacant see.

2. Young clergy dedicated to Constructive Service.

There is always a number of Church folk, especially among the laity, who would like to see the Church become a hybrid of Y.M.C.A. and B.P.O.E., and to these a bishop of similar views is a godsend. They will vote for him early and late, eventually, as a rule, drawing enough votes from the not too extreme High and Low groups to put him over, for he is almost always so willing to genuflect every other second in a Catholic parish or lean familiarly on the communion table in a Protestant center as to be unobjectionable to either side. If, in addition to following St. Paul's advice to be "all things to all men," he has a loud voice and a dramatic manner, his future is assured.

3. Young men with a distinct affinity for the rich, especially rich women. Such men usually marry wealthy wives, and that is an advantage, especially in poor dioceses. Although the ecclesiastical papers flatly denounce as simony the consideration of a prospective bishop's financial resources, there can be no doubt that in numerous cases it counts. And not infrequently these husbands of the rich are very worthy men—and, contrary to popular belief, often much more interested in the welfare of the poor and much more inclined to advanced economic and social views than their less wealthy brethren.

4. To a slighter extent, earnest, able young men full of good works. Naturally, these have a harder time of it in the episcopal elections, but they do get by, chiefly through the influence of godly women. In most dioceses women cannot vote in the council, but their husbands can. And no rich layman, after losing some thousands

73

of dollars in the market through his absence at the diocesan council, wants the additional discomfort of a scene with his pious wife at the dinner table when she learns he failed to vote as she told him to.

Of course, various other types are honored from time to time in the episcopal elections. For example, the Right Rev. Charles Minnigerode Beckwith, late bishop of Alabama, had been a professor of mathematics, but he soon found that mathematical principles are of no avail in governing the Church of God. Attempting to discipline a High Churchman who overrode his authority, he through some ineptitude lost the support of leading Low Churchmen and eventually turned the administration of the diocese completely over to his coadjutor. Another professor—this time of dogmatic theology—the Right Rev. Frederic J. Kinsman, got so much disturbed by the bickerings of the clergy and laity in the Diocese of Delaware that after ten years he resigned his bishopric and entered the Roman Church, where he received various honors but lived as a layman. Nor does an out-and-out Socialist have a happy time of it on the rare occasions when he is chosen to the bishopric. The Right Rev. Paul Jones got along fairly well as ordinary of Utah until the United States entered the World War. Then, insisting on preaching the religion of Jesus instead of that of Woodrow Wilson from the cathedral pulpit, he soon roused the wrath of the "mighty men of the congregation," who appealed to the House of Bishops. That body selected a committee, which pointed out somewhat timorously that Bishop Jones had a right to preach the Gospel of Jesus

74

if he felt he had to, but that "in deference to an excited state of public opinion" it would be wise for him to resign. The House of Bishops, developing—for it—somewhat notable courage, declared it would ask for no bishop's resignation in deference to public opinion. Bishop Jones, being a gentleman, however, realized that he was not wanted and resigned anyway. No Socialist has been elected bishop since.

A NOTE ON THE KANSAS LANGUAGE

Y EARS AGO, when I was a member of the faculty of the Kansas State College, I encountered a talkative farmer on a railway train. Having found out whence I came, he looked at me in open-mouthed admiration and exclaimed:

"That sure is a great school, Perfesser. It's practical. They don't teach no goddam grammar there."

I did not disillusion my acquaintance, but his remarks led me to meditation on the theme of the "Kansas language"—meditation which has not yet, long afterward, reached a definite conclusion, although the term appears day after day in the press of the State and in the addresses of the ardent patriots.

There is no State in which a keener interest is displayed in the minutiæ of grammar. Literary criticism in Kansas—I mean the criticism presented by the sober, old-time Methodist citizens as distinguished from the young iconoclastic devotees of Proust and Franz Kafka — ranks grammar only below moral fervor as a factor in æsthetic evaluation. The Kansas theory of grammar is based on Hoenshel's textbook, possibly the worst work ever written in this field, which was for years the guide, philosopher, and friend of Kansas youth. This book's lack of historical background not improbably accounts for the summary way in which the Kansas Authors Club dropped the apostrophe from the second word in its name. It may also be responsible for the fact that the Poetry Society of Kansas, representing purportedly the *haut ton* of Sunflower letters, devoted the major part of one of its infrequent meetings to the question whether the word *Kansas* could ever be used as an adjective. Such intensity of conviction was manifested that the entire time of the poets' session would have been absorbed had not some one pointed out the importance of discussing an equally poetic subject; to wit, the mimeographing of the club letter.

Again, in no other State do linguistic questions interest newspaper editors to so great an extent. I question if any other newspaper in the world has ever given top-head, front-page position to matters of language as did Major John W. Conway in his editorship of the Norton *Champion*. Nor will one find paragraphers in other States treating of grammatical problems as is done in Kansas, with the same seriousness that is applied to the Gold Standard, the New Deal, and conditions in Soviet Russia.

Yet grammatical differences between the language of Kansans and that of Nebraskans or Iowans are practically non-existent. One observes, here and there, it is true, provincialisms that involve grammar, but upon examination one usually finds that they are importations from the South, New England, the Pennsylvania German sections, or other long-settled regions. There is, however, one usage which I have found so much more frequently here than elsewhere that it may

well be referred to as an integral part of the Kansas
language. That is the use of the past tense of the verb,
as formed with the auxiliary did, instead of the present,
by shopkeepers, waitresses, and others engaged in re-
tail business. It is most exceptional in a Kansas store
to be asked, "What do you wish to see?" Almost invariably the question is, "What *did* you wish to see?"

Historically, the verb thus used is not a past indica-
tive but a subjunctive. The original form was undoubtedly the somewhat tautological "What would you
wish to see?" or the still less direct "What would your
Honor (or your Reverence) wish to see?" The subjunctive was used because the shopkeeper or waitress or
servant considered himself inferior to the person upon
whom he was waiting, and therefore must not address
him directly as an equal would do. The subjunctive
offered the necessary oblique method.

It is curious that in a State which prides itself on
the equality of its citizens the most distinctive expression emphasizes inequality. While the inferiority complex of the more vocal souls expresses itself in boasting
of the glories of Kansas, the general run of folk display
a felt inferiority in the unmeditated use of a servile
phrase.

The Kansas language, if there is such a thing, obviously, then, does not depend on grammar, for one
phrase is surely no more than a single swallow to a linguistic summer. Parenthetically, it should be pointed
out that the phrase, "the Kansas language," is often
enough used today with no linguistic connotation whatever. It is employed by hundreds of politicians to

round out a speech or to avoid the embarrassment of expressing an opinion on a controversial subject. When the hack orator at the political banquet asserts in ringing tones, "My friend, the friend of all of us, that peerless statesman, Congressman Bullwind, is forever dear to this great State because he always and invariably speaks the Kansas language," he means that the noble subject of his panegyric believes in God, the Constitution, the sacredness of American womanhood, the beauty of the Kansas sunset, the peerless quality of Kansas hard winter wheat, the integrity of the Kansas farmer, and the abolition of graft in all places where it is likely to be discovered by the opposing political party. With equal effectiveness Congressman Bullwind himself may reassert, in response to any scurvy trick question, "You know as well as the other citizens of this great State that on that important issue I have always spoken the Kansas language."

Such use of the time-honored expression is, however, quite modern. All is grist that comes to a politician's mill, and the phrase, "the Kansas language," was simply appropriated by local statesmen from its earlier use as referring actually to a style of speech or writing.

Diligent inquiry and reading have failed to uncover the origin of the phrase. William Allen White informs me that he first heard the expression from Noble L. Prentis (1839–1900), and adds that it was common in Prentis's crowd in the seventies and eighties. He suggests the probability of an even earlier origin in the attempt to differentiate Kansas speech from "the

79

oratorical circumlocution and flowery language of the
Southerners who came into Kansas in the fifties and
opposed the Northerners in debate as well as in the
various forms of misdemeanor and felony, which were
habitual in those halcyon days."

No two persons, perhaps, would agree precisely on
a definition of the phrase; it is one of those things
which are felt rather than evaluated intellectually. In
general, "the Kansas language" seems to imply direct-
ness, bluntness, simplicity of speech, with an admixture
of homely and often exceedingly effective humor. It is
notable also for the absence of the bitter, intellectual-
ized wit characteristic of much consciously literary
writing. If one will compare Mr. White's own *What's
the Matter with Kansas?* to my mind the outstanding
example of the Kansas language, with Lowell's *Biglow Papers,* one will at once observe the distinction
that I have mentioned. The *Biglow Papers* are even
less formal than Mr. White's editorial, and quite as
direct. But, whereas the Kansas editor's description of
the Populists would make even an adherent of the
People's party explode into laughter, Lowell's political
comment provokes at most a bitter, cynical smile.

The earliest typical example of the Kansas language
that I have encountered occurs in the *Handbook* of
the Agricultural College for 1874, immediately after
the Rev. John A. Anderson, ex-soldier, printer, politician, Presbyterian minister, became president of the
institution. He succeeded another clergyman, the Rev.
Joseph Denison, D.D., Latinist and student of philosophy, whose principal concession to the farming inter-

ests of the State had been the erection, on an English model, of a barn so big that for years it contained the assembly hall and most of the classrooms. Under Doctor Denison the college catalogue reveled in such lush elegance as this: "The traveler down the valley of the Big Blue, as he gazes upon these cone-like bluffs rising on either side and covered with the verdure of spring, and feels the impression made upon him by the curved lines that bound them, blending with the hues and tints of light and shade that rise around their sides, can scarcely fail to cry out for very joy from the emotions of beauty they awaken."

President Anderson, with his program of education for what he termed "the working classes of Kansas," devoted nearly a hundred pages in his first *Handbook* to a discussion of his principles in the Kansas language.

"If viewed from the standpoint of actual instead of ideal life," he asserted in a characteristic passage, "the average female seminary will logically appear as a standing wonder. . . . The world for which it prepares her (the young woman student) is Dreamland, where the poetic Charles Augustus awaits her arrival that they may sail in a fairy ship over a placid ocean to his castle in Spain, and spend a perpetual youth in delicious wooing while the ceaseless moonlight sifts through overhanging leaves and exotic flowers perfume the air. Charles Augustus is a fraud! His true name is John Smith. He lives in Kansas and earns every cent by hard labor. He tears his clothes, snores, and eats unlimited quantities of pork and cabbage, which Mrs.

John Smith may have to cook, and at the same time
preserve order among an assorted lot of little Smiths,
energetic with mischief and having capacious lungs
and elastic stomachs."

Few other Kansas educators have followed the Rev.
Professor Anderson's style. Nor, for that matter, have
many Kansas statesmen actually used the Kansas language, so called. Even roaring Jim Lane, who boasted
of being self-educated, used to talk sentimentally and
grandiloquently of Kansas as "the Italy of America."
Ingalls was fond of filling his speeches and writings
with words like "catholicon," "plethoric," and "iri-
descent," quite unintelligible to most of his constituents. A number of the Populists, as would be expected,
spoke the Kansas language. Mary Elizabeth Lease
and Jerry Simpson did so with vigor and effectiveness.
But Justice Doster used the language of intellectual
socialism, while Senator Peffer was as dull and statistical as Reed Smoot. Governor Stubbs, leading the Pro-
gressive hosts under the banner of Theodore Roosevelt
and "salt-rising bread," employed the Kansas language.

Not many widely known Kansas writers have used
language distinctive of the State. William Allen
White, of course, has done so, chiefly in political discussion—his fiction, except for some of its subject
matter, might have been written anywhere in the
United States. Among poets Ironquill (Eugene Ware)
stands alone as a user of the Kansas language, and he
employed it only now and then, as in the Bandit's epi-
taph on Ingalls:

Up was he stuck
And in the very upness
Of his stucktitude
He fell.

Who, then, did use the Kansas language? Mainly, newspaper paragraphers and writers of editorials. The term, "the Kansas language," was popularized by Alexander Butts (1844–1910), when he edited the Kansas Notes in the Kansas City *Star* in the late eighties and early nineties. Not only did he use the expression frequently, but he wrote the Kansas language himself and quoted from innumerable newspaper men who also wrote it. The Kansas language undoubtedly was an important factor in keeping the country press of the State from lapsing into either the pompous pretentiousness or the dull sterility characteristic of many editorial pages.

Does the Kansas language now exist as anything but a political phrase? Do people actually write it or speak it? The answer is a matter of opinion. Paul Jones insists that he writes the Kansas language, which he defines as "one-gallus language." Some other editors believe that there is no longer any language typical of the state. The reason for the difference of opinion presumably is that the Kansas language was never a well-defined dialect. If it had been, we should find it in the work of Kansas novelists and poets, as we find Scottish dialect in Burns. Ed. Howe, the most distinguished of Kansas writers, gives the literary approach when he says: "The Kansas language does not greatly differ from the usual English language, but there are differences in life in Kansas and in New York City (or in Pennsylvania, or Louisiana, or California); occasionally it is natural and necessary to give them expression."

The differences to which Mr. Howe refers grow steadily less as life becomes more mechanized and means of transportation and communication increase. Moreover, Kansas has become a conservative State, and most of its people consciously seek to become like the people of other conservative States. Something resembling the old-time Kansas language, as well as the old-time Kansas economics, is more likely to be heard today in Iowa or North Dakota than in Kansas.

Recently, however, the Kansas State Teachers' Association lent its example to the revival of the folk speech of the State. It sponsored in the Wichita *Eagle* an advertisement using the expression, "it's milder pardner" (punctuation and spelling are quoted exactly). It is heartening to note that the pedagogues are setting for us of this effeminate age the spirited example of "no goddam grammar."

WHAT IS NEWSPAPER ENGLISH?

NEWSPAPER MEN and professors of journalism have tried for years to impress the public with the concept of "newspaper English" as a phenomenon that will change the literary history of the world. They have even persuaded high schools to introduce courses under this name. They have convinced most people that contemporary literature and contemporary conversation are based on a peculiar style that reporters have developed.

As to literature, they point out that many notable writers of fiction and verse got early experience on newspapers; ergo, their style must be newspaper style. On examination of the work of such writers, one finds the conclusion unjustified. The ex-journalists who are doing the most distinguished work in fiction and verse in this country are probably Sherwood Anderson, James Branch Cabell, Willa Cather, Theodore Dreiser, Sinclair Lewis, and Carl Sandburg. I should like to have some one show me "newspaper English" in the writings of any of these.

I am aware that Lewis is often referred to as "journalistic." As this is meant, it is a largely undeserved compliment to the profession of journalism. Mr. Lewis is called "journalistic" because he is an accurate, at times photographic, observer. This, it is true, is the ideal of journalism, but it is precisely contrary to the practice of the typical newspaper man. Far from being able to observe complex occurrences with accuracy, he cannot even sit at a copy desk and read with exactitude what comes over it. In a metropolitan daily I recently noticed a head telling of a serious fire in Baltimore. Upon reading the story I found that the fire was in Frederick, which is sixty miles from Baltimore, and that the only connection of the latter city with the fire was that it started in a piece of construction being carried on by a Baltimore firm. As to Mr. Lewis's style, its savage satire would bar it from all but two or three American newspapers. All the writers whom I have mentioned may have got something from newspaper work, but certainly it was not style, "newspaper English."

What, as a matter of fact, is newspaper English?

In the first place, it consists in a certain elegance comparable to that found in the paper-backed novels devoured by London housemaids. This involves the elimination of all words held by managing editors to be "immoral" or "suggestive." For "rape," "incest," or any other word denoting a sexual offense, the editor substitutes "a statutory crime"—which, obviously, means nothing at all. The theory, so managing editors have carefully explained to me, is that young people, who in these days, of course, know nothing about sex, are thus shielded from knowledge of the great world and its evils. The editors follow ardently the journalistic instructions of the sainted Warren Gamaliel Harding, which hang on the wall of many a city room. The final admonition in the code of this great editor follows:

"And, above all, be clean. Never let a dirty word or suggestive story get into type. I want this paper to be so conducted that it can go into any home without destroying the innocence of any child."

Newspaper men are the most sentimental in the world—that is probably why they drink so much—and a managing editor gets more sentimental about what he calls "tiny tots" in the paper than over anything else. His respect for Mr. Harding's moral idealism is increased by his natural affinity for the late President's grammar: "If there is any politics to be played, we will play them in our editorial columns."

Not only does the editor protect the innocence of the child stylistically, as it were. He shields the adult from what he considers "not nice," his standards being approximately those of a soda fountain clerk or a filling station attendant. In a newspaper nothing ever "stinks"; rather, there is "an unpleasant odor." A woman in a news story always "disrobes," never "undresses." I suppose the word "disrobe" is printed elsewhere than in newspapers—certainly in the dictionary —but I have never seen it in any other place so far as I remember, and I have never heard it used by any one except a reformed prostitute married to a rich St. Louis grocer. I have no doubt she learned it in her early career—for she never read anything, even a newspaper—and I strongly suspect journalism got the word from a similar source. After a woman "disrobes," according to the press, she "retires"; she does not "go to bed." I have heard such supposed euphemisms defended by editors in the South as marks of chivalry to the immaculate sex.

Elegance to the newspaper man, however, implies not only moral rectitude—of writing. It must embody also expressions ornate enough to make at least the lowest group of readers gape in bewilderment at such erudition.

The other day, when I drove my car into a repair shop, the mechanic was laboriously reading a newspaper. His perplexed look showed that he had reached an *impasse*. He looked up hopefully at me.

"You're a newspaper man, ain't you, Mr. Crawford?" he asked.

"I used to be," I admitted.

"Well, I'm stuck on this word here." He pointed to "succumb" in a top head.

"Succumb? It means something like 'die,' " I explained.

"Gosh! ain't that word sumpin'? You newspaper fellows sure know some swell language," he concluded, enviously.

With a curious similarity to the peasant point of view, newspapers are prone to reserve for stories of death their phrases of greatest grandeur. "Heat Wave Takes Toll of Fifty" seems to them much more vivid than "Fifty Die From Heat." In the press, as a matter of fact, people rarely "die" from heat—they "expire." In Chicago, gangsters are forever "slumping in their seats" as they are "met with a hail (or a rain) of machine gun bullets." In few cities is a murderer

88

referred to as such, even after he has been convicted. He remains "a slayer"—sometimes, romantically, a "whim slayer" or a "mercy slayer."

Numerous words and constructions are barred from most newspapers for supposed etymological, grammatical, or rhetorical reasons. In this field the most conspicuous—and ridiculous—rule is the one forbidding the use of an adverb between the auxiliary and the principal verb. For example, "he had never spoken" must be altered to "he never had spoken." The rule leads to such manifest absurdities as "the house almost was destroyed"—which I saw in a city daily recently. I have known an editor to rewrite a sentence a dozen times to get rid of a "not" in the verb phrase. Not a few newspaper men with whom I have talked about the banned construction consider that it constitutes splitting an infinitive, and, so far as I have been able to discover, this is the origin of the rule. Early journalists had heard in school or elsewhere that infinitives should not be split. They did not know exactly what constitutes an infinitive and so devised this curious regulation.

The peculiar ignorance of grammar characteristic of even distinguished journalists is illustrated when one of the most conspicuous journalism textbooks lists "a number of" among "adjectives that are commonly misused." Likewise, the author accounts "fewer than" an adverb. And the man who wrote this is far more erudite and experienced than the average newspaper man. Not only has he had varied newspaper experience, but he is a Yale graduate (actually, not in the yellow journal sense) and is author of many books and articles.

Another journalist, who is considered bright enough to conduct a syndicated column of questions and answers in the press, translates *exempli gratia* as "for enough."

A perfectly idiomatic English construction to which newspapers object is the retained object. They insist that "John Goldsmith was given a kick in the rear" is incorrect, and that the sentence should read instead: "A kick in the rear was given to John Goldsmith."

Newspapers criticize justifiably the excessive use of "very." They are not on as solid ground when they bar the use of "partially" for "partly" or "over" for "more than."

Nor are they justified in insisting on the word "today," "this morning," or some similar expression in every news story. This rule, not yet become universal, was devised by the United Press, which, being originally a service for evening papers, thought that the time designation gave readers a stylistic wallop and competitors a financial one. Hence, if the right reverend ordinary of the diocese passes to Paradise at eight o'clock in the evening, the morning daily announces that he "died." The following evening paper, however, gives the altered information that the bishop "today lies dead."

The principal distinction of newspaper English, however, is the use of bizarre expressions, most of them originally figurative, which have become clichés. Journalists often insist that these expressions have been adopted into the conversational language of the people. I have listened for a good while, and I do not discover such words or phrases in the talk of any group. I never hear even newspaper men use them orally. In nobody's conversation, so far as I can ascertain, is a baseball a "spheroid," a member of Congress a "solon," a scientist a "savant," or the pastor of the Third Presbyterian Church a "noted divine."

The journalistic use of such terms comes from three sources. In the first place, the yellow journals from about 1898 on—chiefly those of William Randolph Hearst—were trying to make news vivid to people of limited imagination. Contrary to popular opinion, they did not accomplish their aim chiefly by faking and exaggeration, though they employed these, but by emphasizing the emotional elements in the news. In this process they employed words and phrases that carried, or seemed to carry, emotional connotations, such as "love nest," "prominent clubman," "scantily clad," "crisp bills," "scion of great wealth," "wayward girl," "gruesome sight," "love pirate," "gallant fire fighters," "the unwritten law," "the witness was grilled."

Headlines are a second source of newspaper clichés. The American headline has developed in such a way as to require short words. This accounts for "solons" as a synonym for "legislators," though the ribald may reflect that "boobs" would occupy one less unit of space. It also is responsible for such a head as *Thompson Flays Jones* over an interview in which Committeeman Thompson asserts that Representative Jones voted wrong on the tariff on dried prunes. Most copyreaders today, being cautious and unoriginal, stick to the words that have grown stale through years of head-writing. When they attempt something new, their achievements are as subtle as the antics of a performing bear. For instance, I read several years ago, over a story telling of political criticism of the then President, the head, *Democrats Behead Hoover.* Remembering the influence alleged to be exerted over conversation by newspaper writing, I tried to imagine my barber, my physician, my garage mechanic, or even my friend the statehouse reporter remarking, "Well, I see Thompson flayed Jones today and the Democrats beheaded Hoover."

Another characteristic of the headline that makes for etymological absurdity is the rule that an important word used in one deck of the head must not be used in any other. Consequently, a potato is referred to as a "tuber," an "important root crop," a "million-dollar vegetable,"—and by as many other terms as the length of the head necessitates.

The third main source of the curious expressions that infest journalism is found in the sport pages. When general reporting was stereotyped—as it still is to a large extent—sport writers were given more leeway. Some of the better ones, such as Grantland Rice and Heywood Broun, began writing vividly about baseball, prize fighting, and wrestling. Lesser men tried to follow their example, resulting in the development of a mere jargon, unintelligible except to close followers of sports and never used by them in conversation. Not even the manager of a baseball team talks about "clouting the spheroid," and the average fan feels self-conscious on the rare occasions when he calls his team "the Saints," "the Brewers," or "the Senators," using the nicknames invented by newspaper writers.

In *Essentials in Journalism*, Messrs. Harrington and Frankenberg—professor and press agent respectively —assert optimistically that "there are many misdemeanors in journalism; there is but one crime, that of being dull." Newspaper men generally believe that any one who objects to newspaper English wants the press to be dull, like a late nineteenth-century essay. On the contrary, those newspaper writers who are least dull write something quite different from stereotyped, rule-bound newspaper English. In evidence whereof, let me offer the work of Gerald W. Johnson, Georges Seldes, E. G. Pinkham, Robert Casey, or the late William Bolitho.

LADY COPS IN CAP AND GOWN

ONE DAY RECENTLY, as I was renewing my distant youth on the campus of a mid-Western university, I was buttonholed by a pompous, towering woman who I divined, before she introduced herself, must be the Dean of Women. I tried to escape after muttering a few vacuous commonplaces about the early spring beauty of the spiræa and the coeds, but to no avail.

"Do come into my office," urged the dean. "You are an editor, and I know you are trying to uplift our youth like us educators are."

"Indeed," I put in questioningly.

"Yes, indeed," she went on. "I have always felt that educators and editors were doing God's work as fully as ministers themselves. Sometimes it seems a fruitless task, but we shall have our reward. And so," she added with a grim smile, "will those who offend God's little ones."

By that time we were in her office. She seated herself behind an enormous flat-topped imitation mahogany desk and majestically waved me to a seat facing her.

"Do you know," she said, "you are sitting in the very chair in which hundreds of dear, sweet girls have sobbed out their confessions of loneliness and misplaced trust and sin? And how many of them have gone out, with my kiss upon their lips, resolved to live purer, more unselfish, more consecrated lives."

I recognized the sentence as one quoted to me by a young newspaper reporter purportedly from the good dean's speech before a congress of mothers. To tell the truth, I had not believed the young man, whose gin-drenched breath had led me to suppose he was merely engaging in extemporaneous oratory. Evidently I had misjudged him.

The dean went on. "And here in my desk are the records of the bootleggers whom I have sent to justice, the dance halls that have been closed on my initiative, the vile young men who have been expelled from this university on information that I obtained. And would you believe it, some of them have been among the brightest youths in the whole institution? But they must learn that if God is not in their hearts, their learning is but dust and ashes." (Still more of the young reporter's quotations.)

"I am no criminologist," I put in futilely.

"Of course, of course," the lady assented. "But this subject is so much on my heart. And it does lead to something that I wanted to tell you about. For a number of years we have had the custom in the university of not permitting students to return if they fail to pass in half their work."

"A fine idea," I assented with enthusiasm. "It saves the professor's time and the taxpayers' money."

"Oh, but I'm afraid you don't understand. I have known hundreds of dear, sweet girls and fine, upstanding boys who were dropped from college for that reason. Students who were active in Y.M.C.A., the Y.M.C.A., and have been a great influence in their fraternities and sororities. Only three years ago there was a boy who almost single-handed kept liquor out of his fraternity house, and the faculty wouldn't let him enrol again because he had failed in his studies. Why, as I told them, the poor boy was just too busy to give the time to his school work. Now he is working in a filling station, and he might, if the university had encouraged him—he might have become a second Billy Sunday.

"But that is going to be changed. I tell you, Mr. Crawford, the depression has done some good, right here in this university. Our enrolment dropped down, and the president and faculty knew we had to do something to appease the legislature. So I proposed that we write to all these boys and girls that we haven't let enrol and tell them they could come back, provided there was nothing wrong with them except their studies. I told the faculty how it would increase the enrolment and how these boys and girls, who haven't any jobs, would come gack here and get an education. And they voted to do it. There was a good deal of opposition, but my side won. Education is the hope of the world," she concluded in a magnificent *non sequitur*, "or else ignorance is."

"Perhaps it is," I remarked in a subdued tone.

"I knew you would agree with me," she said magnanimously.

The ubiquity of deans of women in American colleges today causes the casual observer to forget that they are a comparatively recent development in the dedication of the nation to high-powered pedagogy. The deans themselves trace the origin of their office to the appointment of Alice Freeman Palmer at the founding of the University of Chicago in 1892. Strictly speaking, Mrs. Palmer was not a dean of women in the contemporary sense of the term. The University of Chicago was abandoning a precedent of important privately endowed institutions in adopting coeducation, and Mrs. Palmer was made "dean of the women's department." She served for three years, and, being a woman of taste and culture, she offered sound advice and example to the none too well-trained young women who enrolled in the university in its early days.

Her success led the presidents of other institutions, always ambitious for educational novelty, to appoint deans of women. The movement grew rapidly in the universities—especially the State institutions, where the selection of a pious Methodist or Baptist woman offered an excellent way to appease the wrath of the evangelical clergy over the teaching of evolution and the immoral clothes of the university girls. The smaller colleges, never to be outdone in zeal for right-eousness, likewise appointed deans of women. In these instances the individual chosen was often the lady professor of the Bible or the wife of the leading local pastor. In the agricultural colleges, whose female students in those days were mostly taking home economics, the head of this department was frequently given the duties of dean of women also, so that she might teach the girls how to behave themselves in a hammock as well as how

97

to eat peas with a fork and how to make sandwiches out of nasturtium stems. Even some up-and-coming business colleges employed deans of women.

The deans, like other pedagogues, were not content with their success. Fired with a noble discontent, they inaugurated a movement to establish the office of dean of girls in the high schools. The National Association of Deans of Women once announced as one of its primary objects "to make clear to the public and to governing boards of educational institutions where girls and women are educated, the necessity of having in each of these institutions a competent and thoroughly trained woman as dean of women, or of girls." The tax-paying public, however, reacted somewhat unfavorably to this frank avowal, and in 1932 the association dropped the statement by a majority of one vote. A large number of deans of women continue to work for establishment of their office in every high school. The propaganda is carried on chiefly through the State Federations of Women's Clubs. The mothers in these organizations are frightened by dire tales of what may be happening to their daughters in any school that is not kept in God's path by a lady dean, while the spinsters are pleasantly titillated by the same stories. The result is grandiloquent resolutions and pressure upon boards of education. The superintendent of schools can almost invariably be counted on to back the scheme both because of his hospitality to every educational nicknack and his constant interest in increasing the number of his employés.

Eventually, one may presume, there will be deans of

girls for the elementary schools and deans of babies for the nursery schools. The busy city of Bristow, Oklahoma—population, 6,619—has already made a start in this direction by naming a dean of girls for the entire public school system.

The Association of Deans of Women has approximately 1,100 members, only one-third of whom, notwithstanding the barrage of propaganda, are connected with high schools. There of course are a number of deans that do not belong to the organization. Inasmuch as there are only about 600 standard colleges in the United States, the rest of the deans are accounted for chiefly by junior colleges and by the fact that two or more women in a single institution often are engaged in work entitling them to membership in the association. For instance, the Iowa State College of Agriculture and Mechanic Arts has not been content with a dean of women but has employed a director of housing, a director of social life, and a director of personnel, each presumably with her appropriate quota of secretaries, stengraphers, typists, messengers, publicity experts, and confidential agents.

The typical dean of women must not be confused with scholars like Dr. Marjorie Hope Nicolson of Smith College or Dr. Virginia Crocheron Gildersleeve of Barnard College. These women, intellectual and civilized, are responsible officials of their institutions, comparable in function to the dean of the college of liberal arts in any great university. Between them and the usual dean of women in a co-educational institution there is as wide a gulf as between the chancellor of the

University of Louvain and a hedgerow priest teaching Mexican peons that God disapproves of murder. There are, it is true, young, intelligent, and well-educated women acting as deans of women in all sorts of colleges and universities here and there over the country, but they are in a minority. So are those deans whose primary duty is to teach a subject in which they are specialists but who have been selected, because of outstanding ability as advisers, to devote a small proportion of their time to counseling young women students.

According to the United States Department of Education's *Survey of Land-Grant Colleges and Universities,* published in 1930, five of the thirty-nine institutions reporting showed no academic training for the dean of women. One of the remainder proudly boasted that its dean was a graduate nurse. Since the land-grant colleges are far above the average in resources, an examination of the qualifications of deans of women in all American institutions would doubtless present an even less flattering picture. The typical dean of women is either a professor whom the president of the college has thus shelved in his anxiety to remove her from teaching duties or a motherly-looking old lady who can be counted on to impress moronic voters or prospective contributors with the moral wholesomeness of the institution. Most of the deans are aged and grow constantly more pompous in office, like bishops whose rings are kissed by throngs of the pious.

The deans have nearly all become convinced that theirs is a great profession, ranking with those of city superintendent of schools, compiler of "intelligence" tests, and professor of educational measurements. They encourage young women who otherwise would become Y.W.C.A. secretaries or wives of ministers, to prepare themselves for deanships. Several institutions advertise elaborate courses in this direction. The most extensive work, as would be expected, is given by Teachers' College of Columbia University. This institution offers a diploma bearing the proud title, Dean of Women, or Dean of Girls. In preparation for this distinguished honor the student follows such courses as Student Personnel Administration, Educational Administration, Introduction to Research in Educational Guidance, Research in Educational Guidance, Field Course in Educational and Social Guidance, Student Residence Halls, Problems of Student Advisement, and Personnel Techniques and Their Use in Personnel Administration. The University of Chicago goes in for "the case-history methods of studying girls," but apparently requires no economic or psychiatric preparation for this study. The general run of institutions lag behind these leaders. Typical is the Colorado State Teachers' College, which merely lists a course in Women in Administration along with such other educational titbits as Schoolhouse Construction, Great Personalities of the Old Testament, School Publicity, and Boy Scout Work.

Acceptance of standards of academic education by many of the deans is, however, grudging at best. Feeling that they are working under the inspiration of the Holy Spirit, they resent the implication that their work would be benefited by a knowledge of psychology, grammar, economics, and other worldly subjects. In

1929 and again in 1930 an effort was made by the intelligentsia of the order to restrict membership in the national organization to women holding at least a bachelor's degree from a college accredited by the Association of American Universities. Notwithstanding the rule was carefully worded to preserve the membership of any one already in the organization, it was turned down.

The prevailing level of intellectual curiosity in the profession is illustrated by a report of the Committee on Intellectual and Educational Policies, which included the lofty suggestion that a dean contribute to the intellectual life of her institution by joining 'the Book-of-the-Month Club. When the deans go in for literature of their own, as in formal addresses and essays, they reach equal heights of profundity, as illustrated in these significant examples of philosophy, rhetoric, and grammar respectively:

"What men know, women soon discover, and soon reflections of wrong habits of mind and habit become increasingly evident among college women."—Ethel Chase, College of the City of Detroit.

"A lovely initiation service is worked out on the idea of the Greek goddess presiding over each group."— Hazel Prutsman Schwering, University of Oregon.

"Whether we study marriage failures or marriage successes, we have statistical evidence that possession of, or lack of, common interests and common tastes are fundamental determinants. The co-educational institutions, which seven-eighths of our women students attend, afford excellent and many opportunities for meeting and knowing persons of similar tastes."—Mrs. Ernestine Cookson Miller, Guilford College.

Some of the deans, it is true, have aspirations— vicarious at least—toward literary culture. One whom I used to know consulted me as to the chance of making "an important writer, like Harold Bell Wright," of her collegiate son, whose mental age I should estimate was about thirteen years. When the lad at last became a hairbrush salesman, the world, in her judgment, lost a potential literary genius. Another, serving on a library committee, wanted to display her linguistic knowledge and offered to recommend foreign books. Ordering Goethe's "Sämtliche Werke," she was astonished, when the set came, to find that it was not a single volume. "And it contains *Faust*," she exclaimed. "I had thought it was one of his *other* poems."

When a dean of women actually writes a book, the entire order rejoices. For years Dr. Frances Louise Nardin, dean of women in the University of Wisconsin, was noted by the deans as a great literary light because of her authorship of *The Progress of Liberty*, *The Bugle Calls the Children*, *Makers of America—A Civic Ritual*, and other patriotic sublimities. Since her retirement no distinguished æsthetic figure has arisen among the deans.

The duties of a dean of women are no more specifically defined than those of a minister in the average Protestant denomination. Like the minister, she is employed vaguely to do good. The result is that she constantly hunts for good deeds to perform, and, conversely, for evils to stamp out. The average dean finds

103

many more of the latter than of the former. Among deans' duties are likely to be supervision of sorority chapters, inspection of rooming houses, excusing of absences, membership on all faculty committees having anything to do with women students, regulation of dances, chaperonage of picnics, regulation of the use of automobiles, setting of study hours, regulation of women's athletics, decision as to how many offices a girl may hold in student organization, censorship of the lines and costumes in college plays, propaganda for the Y.W.C.A. (along with efforts to prevent its becoming socialistic), and, most important of all, advice to all the girls and stern discipline for those who transgress the multitudinous rules that the dean has laid down. In a few institutions the dean of women has complete control of the curriculum to be pursued by the co-eds on the theory that otherwise the girls would impair their health through overstudy or injure their morals by learning facts that women do not need to know. A number of the deans feel that they should have similar control in every institution.

In some of the more enlightened universities the dean's duties are severely restricted by university statute, in which case she becomes chiefly a consultant to women who seek her advice and to the faculty when it deals with problems concerned with women students. Likewise some deans, in the absence of any such restriction, adopt a similar policy themselves. These are mostly younger and better-trained women, many of them possessing knowledge of psychiatry and social psychology. Their number is increasing but it still is very small. The average dean resembles a Methodist minister elevated to be sheriff of his county and provided with an inexhaustible supply of blank warrants.

Each year she gathers the freshman girls together for weekly meetings of prophylaxis. Liquor and tobacco, she warns the young things, are powerful aphrodisiacs, and not only must the righteous young woman abstain from them, but she must refuse to accept the escort of any youth whose breath suggests gin or whisky. More than that, if she is a genuine Christian, she will come to the dean and tell his name, so that he may be punished by the university.

Also, she explains that certain perfumes are exciting to young men and that godly girls no more think of using these fragrances than of receiving company in their nighties. A friend of mine, a druggist in a university town, possesses the list of perfumes, and at the beginning of each academic year puts in a sufficient supply for two-thirds of the freshman girls. By the sophomore year, he tells me, the young women have discovered more effectual means of attracting worthy young men.

Likewise the deans suggest what magazines to carry in order to appear both intelligent and modest. A similar impression, they point out, may be made in the selection of picture shows. Some deans even give lists of words that should be avoided in conversation with young men. In one of the largest universities in America, the dean solemnly warned her protégées never to use the word *soup*, which she insisted so puckered the

105

lips as to impel any man to a kiss. To show her girls how ladies and gentlemen should act when together, Miss Martha Reid, dean of women in the University of Arkansas, persuaded the members of the Fayetteville Chamber of Commerce to take the freshman girls motoring on Sunday afternoons. In late years the bolder spirits have ventured into discussion of sex hygiene. Prof. Sue C. Hamilton of Ferry Hall is one of those. When some of the other deans, intrigued yet apprehensive, asked where she got her material, she replied, "From here, there, and everywhere, from the *Chicago Tribune* to the Bible."

The deans constantly watch the members of the faculty, especially the younger, more personable, or more radical men, for traces of evil influence upon their charges. They are in perpetual anxiety over the courses in psychology, economics, and literature. The young men who teach psychology are likely to be behaviorists, Freudians, or disciples of the *Gestalt* school. Modern economics, they are sure, will cause the girls to substitute Karl Marx for the Old Testament Divinity and to abandon the notion that marriages are made in Heaven.

As for literature, why, they plaintively ask, should pure-minded young women be required to read immoral and depressing books when there exist the works of Gene Stratton-Porter, Ruby M. Ayres, and Temple Bailey? In some of the more sophisticated universities they are laughed down, but in the less enlightened institutions they have real power. Through their influence, in some places an expurgated edition of Chaucer's

106

Prologue to the *Canterbury Tales* is used in which there is omitted even the line:

"I trowe he were a gelding or a mare."

Likewise, they have introduced Bourdillon's translation of *Aucasin e Nicolete*, wherein the lovely lady, quite contrary to the Old French original, shows barely her ankle to the bedfast palmer.

The lady dean formally protested in a certain university against the study of John Ford's well-known play, " 'Tis Pity She's a Whore," in an advanced course in English literature.

"The word is in the Bible. That ought to be good enough for you," answered the professor, a gruff bearded scholar with no taste for meddlesome women.

The dean was taken aback. She hesitated, then recovered herself.

"I'm sure it was not in the Bible that I studied under dear old Dr. Bland in Arkansas," she replied with dignity. "He invariably said, 'bad woman.' These new translations of the Bible are influenced by such men as Sherwood Anderson and Eugene O'Neill."

When they have censored the courses, the lady deans' multitudinous responsibilities are still left undischarged. The young women must be guarded against the seductive wiles of attractive instructors, and frequently they are warned to leave the outer door open when they enter a professor's office.

On the other hand, I have known tactful young men on college faculties to attain academic promotion through a discreet kiss implanted on the lips of a dean while sitting in a dark corner of a veranda during a

107

fraternity dance. Such projects are not to be undertaken lightly, however. Once a male student, more impetuous than wise, was compelled to take a vacation from his college because he seized the dean, whom he mistook one night on a garden path for a favorite student, and gave her a severe necking.

No small part of the average dean's time is spent in ferreting out evil, ranging from sexual delinquency to offenses against the majesty of the dean; to wit, violations of the rules that she has laid down or has persuaded a council of faculty or students to adopt. In her activities she often has the ready assistance of the dean of men—in institutions unfortunate enough to have such a functionary. The dean of women, esteeming herself a lady, must refrain from visiting some of the places where the more vivid sins are most likely to be discovered. The dean of men, however, can sit for ten hours in a parked car on a hillside or can go into a saloon or a fraternity house, plant himself in the best chair, and stare grimly at his surroundings all night like a cop awaiting a counterfeiter. The dean of women must content herself with her colleague's recital of what he sees. Once she has learned the worst, however, she is even more ardent than he in seeking condign punishment for the offenders. Occasionally, after being thoroughly frightened, a culprit is allowed to go free on condition that she inform the dean of all future highjinks of which she learns. This method, of course, is borrowed from the practice of metropolitan police and the now obsolete schemes of federal prohibition officers.

The overwhelming majority of offenses with which the dean of women is concerned are violations neither of statutory law nor of the ordinary practices of semi-civilized Americans, to which class the deans generally belong. One college has a rule that no couple walking into the country may carry a blanket. Another institution prescribes the number of watts of electric light per square foot of space on the dance floor. Still another requires that girls be in their rooms between 2:45 and 6 A.M. after farewell fraternity parties.

Mrs. Geraldine Green, of the West Texas State Teachers' College, one of the lights of the Association of Deans of Women, compiled a list of offenses in thirty-three institutions in one month. This is the lamentable record:

Nature of Offense	Total of Offenses
Automobiling without permission	29
Out after lights	26
Dancing too late	20
Attending dances without permission	19
Disturbing class, assembly, or boarding house	18
Smoking	16
Failure to attend classes	15
Disregard for all regulations	9
Cheating	9
Rude to matron	7
Disregard of courtesies	7
Improper clothes	7
Drinking	7
Out without permission	6
Psychiatric cases	5

Nature of Offense	Total of Offenses
Excessive use of cosmetics	5
Improper masquerade clothes	5
Moving without permission	5
Impudence	5
Sitting out in cars	4
Theft, or borrowing without return	4
Pursuing young men	4
On street too much	4
Petting	4
Too many dates	4
Visiting men's boarding houses	4
Trouble maker	3
Water throwing	2
Going into other girls' rooms	2
Student working for board—unsatisfactory	2
Gave incorrect destination on permit	2
Misinterpretation of standards	2
Indifference	2
Refusal to study	2
Refusal to eat	1
Overdue library books	1
Girl married—did not tell householder	1
Bad checks	1
Refusal to pay debts	1
Dispute over guest privileges	1
Untidiness—carelessness in bath	1
Suspected drinking	1
Entertained company too late	1
Too many parental visitors on study nights	1

Now and then an irate student or her father rises in wrath against the efforts of a dean to impose the

110

standards of 1895. In such a case the dean feels as insulted as a professor of mathematics accused of not knowing how to add, but often she backs down after delivering an adequate warning of failure in this life and punishment in the hereafter.

Notwithstanding their distaste for a vigorous fight, the spirits of the deans have been illumined and stimulated by two judicial decisions; indeed, one can hardly talk for five minutes to one of them without hearing a reference to "those splendid, God-fearing judges."

Michigan furnished the first example of godliness in the judiciary. The plaintiff was a young woman in the Michigan State Normal College at Ypsilanti. She had been used to smoking at home, and, Ypsilanti seeming homelike, she saw no reason for not lighting a cigaret there. Unluckily the stern and Puritan dean of women caught her in the act. Not only was she smoking, but she was sitting in the lap of a personable young man in the front seat of a motor car. Most of the serious-minded young women who attend teachers' colleges are of a type not invited into the cars—or laps—of good-looking boys, and the dean could hardly believe her eyes. But she looked more closely and was convinced. She ran as fast as a perfect lady should to the office of the president of the institution, Professor Charles McKenny, LL.D. (Olivet), D. Ed. (Miami), author of *The Personality of the Teacher*. Promptly he agreed with the dean that the cigaret-smoking young woman had not the personality that he idealized in his book; with many a *tsk, tsk*, the two educators determined that she should not enrol for the following term.

They called the culprit in, and told her their decision. They had expected her to burst into tears, promise to be a sweet girl, and never more to touch a cigaret or sit within a foot of a boy in a motor car. Instead, she flounced out of the office, walked down the street to the local newspaper office, and wrote a scathing letter about prudes. Taken aback by this but not yet discouraged, the professors demanded the presence of her older sister, a resident of the town, who they trusted would put the smart young thing in her place. But again they were disappointed. All that the sister did was to coöperate in supplying adjectives for further letters to the press. Finally, the young woman sued for reinstatement in the college.

The lower court decided against her, whereupon she immediately appealed to the supreme court. There, to the joy of all deans of women, she lost again. Newspaper men and other ribald souls through the state had poked fun at the college, but now the tables were turned. No less a figure than the Hon. Grant Fellows, elderly bachelor now gone to his rest, wrote the decision, affixing to it this coda:

"Instead of condemning [the dean], she should be commended for upholding some old-fashioned ideals of young womanhood."

The good Dr. McKenny, advanced in years, rested serene in the consciousness of having done his duty; he needed no further reward. But the dean promptly became the heroine of the deans of women of the entire country. Nor was she without material reward. From presiding over the girls in a little teachers' college, she was promoted to the deanship of women at a great State university.

Other deans envy this distinguished figure her brush with Satan, and look forward hopefully to the time when her ideals shall be established by law in every educational institution. "This was a teachers' college," remarked Mary Ross Potter, counselor for women, Northwestern University, in a public address. "But shall the school which aspires to develop its students along broader lines than those of a single profession, and send them forth with a foundation for any honorable walk in life, be satisfied with something short of the fine sense of values which, in the cold eye of the law, the teacher should have?"

The other epoch-making decision to which the deans constantly refer was rendered by the Montana Supreme Court and written by Justice Albert Philander Stark, Methodist, Elk, and Kiwanian. In this instance Mrs. Janet T. Ingersoll, one of the most brilliant students in the University of Montana, constantly on the institution's scholarship honor roll, was summarily suspended, along with her husband, on the vague ground that they exerted "a wrong influence on the campus." It seems that they let other students come to their house unchaperoned by any one approved by the dean of women, and some of these youths would sometimes take a drink from a hip flask. The height of Mrs. Ingersoll's bad influence, in the mind of the good dean, came when she admitted to her home, late in the evening, a young woman who already had had a few drinks too many. Obviously, in the judgment of any right-think-ing dean, Mrs. Ingersoll should have slammed the door in her face and let her wander about in the zero weather of Missoula.

Mrs. Ingersoll, moreover, proved recalcitrant when the dean interviewed her. She stated that she did not drink herself, but declined to give the names of her guests or any information as to their tastes or habits. Worse, when she was dismissed, she sued the president, Dr. Charles H. Clapp, an authority on geology more than on deans, and the dean of women, Prof. Harriet R. Sedman, for reinstatement. The case went against her, the court holding that the university did not need to give a student anything in the nature of a judicial hearing. A dissenting opinion was filed, however, by Justice Albert John Galen declaring that the academic authorities had acted on "prejudices . . . gossip admittedly baseless . . . the rankest kind of hearsay evidence." "A case of this character," he concluded, "should never be before the courts, and would not therein be given serious consideration were administrative officers disposed to perform their simple duty in the premises."

But the deans maintain that the majority opinions of appellate courts, plus their own consciousness that the God of Queen Victoria guides them, are assurance enough that they are doing their duty to "the dear young women who will be the future mothers of the race."

THE NOBILITY OF THE CAMPUS

AT A FRONTIER STATE UNIVERSITY, members of the principal fraternity on the campus were calling at the new home of a sorority. With the fraternity youths was one of their pledges, a lad a little older than most freshmen, who, after working a couple of years as an oil driller, had got an interest in a lease, had struck a gusher, and immediately had started for college to acquire the culture that he had often seen on exhibit among the university boys and girls gathered in vacations at the oil-town drug store.

The girls began showing the boys through the house. They inspected the basement with its gas furnace, stationary tubs, chapter hall, and other modern necessities. On the main floor they saw the double living-room with its dimly lighted cozy corners, the dining-room, the library—containing Baird's *Manual of College Fraternities*, a half dozen copies of *College Humor*, and Emily Post on etiquette—and the kitchen.

Then they started for the second floor. The ex-driller, who had been looking more and more puzzled as the tour proceeded, hung back. The president of the sorority noticed him, and mindful of how Mrs. Post would act under like circumstances, came back and engaged him in conversation.

"I wonder if you wouldn't like to see the rest of our house. It's quite"—she thought Mrs. Post would have said *au fait*, but she still was too close to the farm to be sure of her French, so she concluded lamely, "quite cozy."

"No, ma'am, thank you," answered the youth. "I don't believe I will."

"I wish you would," insisted the girl. "All the other boys have gone up, and you're going to be one of them."

The young man was still more obviously embarrassed. "I just don't think I will tonight," he said blushing.

The sorority president felt that her reputation as a hostess was at stake. She remembered that the etiquette book said something about "laying your cards on the table," though she wasn't sure but that was a literal reference to claiming the remaining tricks in bridge. She plunged with a direct question.

"Won't you please tell me why you don't want to go with the other boys? If you'll tell me, perhaps I can do something about it. You make me feel that our house isn't hospitable to you."

The youth gulped, then blurted out, "Well, to tell you the God's truth, I changed my clothes before I came, and I haven't a cent of money in my pocket. Would you take a check?"

From such material the American college fraternity develops throngs of young men who—while they may know little about humanism or the ether drift—can mix a dubious cocktail according to a collegiate formula, can converse with young women about favorite talkies and motor-cars, and can wear clothes of the same quality and with almost the same assurance as a metropolitan gangster.

The fraternities make a great to-do about what they term "fraternity material." One of the national orders will enter Stringtown College, because, although already eighty per cent of its students are fraternity men, it has in the remaining twenty per cent an abundance of "fraternity material." It will stay out of Penguin University, which with only one-fourth of its students wearing gold and enameled pins, hasn't any more "fraternity material" available. The phrase is defined by the brethren in terms of sportsmanship, loyalty, ability, character, and ideals, in the vague language employed by politicians in nominating candidates for office.

Realistically it is something else. The eighty national college fraternities in the United States differ somewhat in their interpretation of "fraternity material," otherwise they would be exactly alike. A number—chiefly younger organizations with an inferiority complex—rigidly exclude Jews. Several admit none but Jews to membership. At least one, Alpha Chi Rho, restricts its roster to "professing Christians," and as a matter of fact has strong Anglican leanings. Phi Kappa is confined to Roman Catholics. The Masons are represented by Acacia, and the Order of De Molay by Delta Sigma Lambda, while even the Odd Fellows used to have a collegiate order, Phi Lambda Theta. In 1924, however, this fraternity cut loose from its papa and has since pursued an independent career, though with only six chapters. The Negroes have sev-

117

eral fraternities. Alpha Gamma Rho refuses to admit anybody who is not a student of agriculture, and in true granger fashion carries a sheaf and a sickle on its badge. The conspicuous sickle, however, has so often caused near-sighted Communists to mistake Alpha Gams for Soviet brothers that these sterling farm boys, when they visit New York City, no longer venture into East Fourteenth Street cafés. A very few old fraternities pride themselves on small chapters, but many of the noble orders would rival the Eagles or the Knights of Pythias in size if they could. Sigma Alpha Epsilon boasts of one chapter containing 110 members.

Outside these differences, fraternities in most institutions set up about the same qualifications for membership. Foremost is cash. Thirty years ago attractiveness to the girls stood first, and finances second. A favorite fraternity song of those days described the perfect pledge:

"He was handsome and so was a pet with the girls
And of cash his pa had a mint."

Today these are reversed, or rather the former is hardly considered at all. The boys know well that any man with enough ready money will get consideration from the beautiful coeds and college widows.

It costs money to run a fraternity chapter. According to last reports, about 2,000 houses were owned by chapters. Some of these, of course, are small and unpretentious. An increasing number, however, are large and costly, and there is intense rivalry on many a campus as to which fraternity shall have the

118

most expensive building. Naturally, the younger organizations are most anxious to make a showing, and they spend the most money. The average value of the houses of Kappa Alpha, which was founded in 1825 and occupies an outstanding position, is less than $40,000, while Alpha Epsilon Pi, founded in 1913, has a group of chapter houses worth $51,000 apiece. Of course, there are exceptions. Delta Psi, more than eighty years old, has the most costly houses of any fraternity. Two of these, however, were given outright by millionaire members of the fraternity, which represents the wealthiest and most fashionable membership among college organizations.

When the alumni buy the house, the active chapter is not so pressed for cash as when it has built the edifice on borrowed capital. In either event, however, it must keep the house going, as alumni, however rich and loyal, are seldom willing to contribute toward the running expenses of the chapter. Hence the necessity for rich freshmen—and plenty of them. If rich boys can be got who can eat soup noiselessly and dance without ruining every satin slipper on the floor, so much the better. If not, the chapter will undertake to train them. Not a few of the less literate chapters have had to introduce systems of fines, which not only promote manners but add copiously to the treasury. For instance:

Late at meals, 10 cents.
Spilling gravy, 5 cents.
Reaching for articles, 5 cents.
Dipping bread in coffee, 15 cents.

119

Wiping nose with napkin, 20 cents.
Eating with knife, 20 cents.
Whistling at the table, 25 cents.
Singing at the table (except fraternity hymns
in concert), 50 cents.
Drinking from saucer, 75 cents.

An occasional rich youth from a mining region or from the family of a newly arrived motion picture magnate can thus sometimes be charged a couple of dollars a meal for several weeks in addition to his regular board.

In selecting members, next to the wealthy young men come the relatives—sons, grandsons, brothers, nephews, and first, second, third, and fourth cousins— of the alumni. These have to be considered, regardless of the feelings of the active chapter, because no chapter is anxious to offend the old grads, particularly if the latter are well supplied with cash. Some fraternities—mostly the older and more conservative ones —have a tradition that boys recommended by relatives shall be elected to membership, unless they show some outstanding and easily demonstrable disqualification. In some instances, of course, such an individual is actually *persona non grata*, but he is voted in anyhow and is accepted by the boys as a visitation of an inscrutable Providence.

Even lacking such a tradition, most chapters hesitate before turning down the immediate relative of an alumnus, particularly if he was a member of the same chapter. When they do not show some deference, there is trouble. In one instance of which I know, a prominent lawyer, a charter member of a certain chapter, sent his son back to dear old *alma mater*. A letter to the fraternity chapter had preceded him. The boys did not even trouble to look the youth up. He wrote to Dad, expressing his indignation and incidentally retailing the campus gossip about the doings of the chapter. The old man was wroth. In his best legal language, he wrote to the national president of the fraternity, telling him all that Son had said of the chapter's standing and adding a lot of other insinuations.

Within a week, two of the national officers were on the campus. They did a little sleuthing of their own, then called one afternoon at the chapter house. An awkward youth came to the door.

"We are Brothers Thompson and Burwell," said one of the callers. "We should like to see Brother Jenkins, the president of your chapter."

"I'll see if he's here," replied the freshman, leaving them standing at the door.

In a few moments he returned. "Jenkins is playing cards," he said. "You can come in and wait if you want to."

The officers entered, seated themselves, and waited. An hour, an hour and a half, two hours, elapsed, with the dignitaries getting constantly madder. When the card-playing president finally came downstairs, they introduced themselves formally, then told him in well-chosen words exactly what the chapter must do if they were not to suspend its charter immediately. Among other things the chapter must bring before the officers that very evening all pledges and all men who were

121

being considered for pledging, to be personally approved by the national functionaries. The chapter president humbly agreed. In the meantime he bethought himself of the freshman about which the out-of-town lawyer had written. Maybe it would be well to have the son of an alumnus present. He called the youth on the telephone and invited him to dinner. The boy hesitated, but finally consented to come. The president himself called for him at his dormitory. The lad was wearing the pledge pin of another organization, and what was the president's chagrin, at the end of the evening, to hear the national secretary say, "You are the worst bunch of nitwits I have ever met. That kid who's pledged to the Rho Phis is the best boy you had here." All that the local president had to console himself was the fact that the national officers didn't take the charter away with them.

In still other ways alumni can be a great bother. One of the leading Christian workers of the country, who goes among the colleges scaring the boys with stories about delirium tremens and syphilis, seasoned with incidents from his own naughty past, belongs to a prominent fraternity. He always looks up the local chapter wherever he goes and in addition makes inquiries about its reputation for moral and religious zeal. Often he sends vigorous and uncomplimentary reports to the national officers. If, however, the members attend his meetings, sitting in a body on the front row, all is well. He will stop in the midst of his prepared speech to call the attention of the audience to "that fine group of upstanding young men whose fraternity I, through the providence of God, was led to join years ago."

After one such meeting, a ribald scoffer in the chapter bought an enormous bouquet of violets and sent it to the Christian evangelist's hotel with a card reading, "With love from your brothers and gratitude for your darling reference to our chapter. We have not been so thrilled since Aimée Semple McPherson was here." Late that night, the young man got tight and began to boast of his gift to the reforming brother. The other members of the chapter were alarmed and started for the hotel, with the idea of apologizing to the evangelist and ducking the atheistic brother in the pond on their return. They found that the Christian worker had left town, so they contented themselves with executing judgment on the sender of the flowers. What was their surprise, upon returning to the chapter house, to find a special delivery letter from the evangelist, full of lyrical praise of the chapter, including an especially lush reference to "the touching and beautiful tribute of affection which came just as I was leaving." "It has heartened me in God's work," he continued. "The Lord will reward you."

Lest the Lord should be forgetful, the evangelist himself sent a long letter to the national president of the fraternity, pointing out that there was the best chapter of any organization that he had ever encountered in his long experience in colleges.

A worse burden are the alumni who have become consciously superior to fraternities since leaving college. While Woodrow Wilson lived, it was a deep

123

humiliation to the Phi Kappa Psis, who claimed him as their most illustrious brother, to have to admit that he was opposed to college fraternities altogether. On the other hand, there are numerous alumni who are quite ideal in the opinion of the undergraduates. They appear at football games with quantities of excellent liquor, which they share freely. They can always be touched for a loan or a contribution. They are childless, or have only beautiful and seductive daughters, whom they are happy to introduce to the members of the order. They never recommend for membership a lad who does not conform exactly to what the active boys proudly call "our type."

When wealth and alumni influence are disposed of, it usually is still necessary to elect some more brethren to fill up the house and help pay expenses. The choice is customarily made, to begin with, from those who were prominent in "activities" in high school and therefore may be expected to adopt the same policy in college. Activities comprise anything non-scholastic from writing a class poem to being fullback on the football team, but naturally football and saxophone players are preferred to poets.

Scholarship is rarely considered. In most of the larger institutions the standing of the fraternity men is notoriously lower than the average of the student body. The national officers of almost all the fraternities have in late years made strenuous efforts to raise the scholastic standing of their chapters, and by dint of threats and ridicule have had some success. In not a few cases, however, the local chapters, when the na-

124

tional officers make things too warm, take care of the situation by electing to membership half a dozen non-fraternity seniors who will make Phi Beta Kappa. These men will raise the standard of the chapter to a glorious height, while they will not bother the other members by living at the house or taking any more active part in affairs than attending an occasional dance or business meeting. There are, it is true, notable exceptions—chapters which are made up of scholarly and cultivated young men. But they are not numerous, and they do not attain much campus reputation. Several years ago, a secret vote was taken in one of the most prominent of American colleges as to the rank of the various chapters in the minds of the students themselves. The three chapters voted to be best were the three which ranked lowest in scholarship in the whole list.

The fraternities insist that instead of grinds, they prefer men who will make good in later life. All investigations—and numerous ones have been made—show, nevertheless, a high correlation between scholastic standing and success in professional or business life, whether it be engineering, selling bonds, editing, practicing law, or what not.

Once a boy is elected to membership in a fraternity and puts on the pledge button, the fraternity endeavors to mold him to what it considers its type. Not only does it regulate his eating habits, but it teaches him what clothes are smart, how to wear his hair, what risqué stories are proper to tell the girls, and how to say "Yeah?" with the right inflection. The fraternity

125

gives him access to the store of foreign language ponies kept in the house and also to the supply of themes written by brothers in past years and given high grades by instructors. If in a coeducational institution, it points out to him that he should seldom "date" a girl who is not a sorority member and never a girl who is earning her way in college by stenography or any other useful trade. It insists on his taking part in college "activities." Certain chapters require that each pledge take part in a specific number, usually from three to five.

The brothers also teach him the Greek alphabet and require him to commit to memory a mass of data about the fraternity and its chapters. They also try to instruct him in bridge, but in this they ordinarily are unsuccessful, for they seldom know anything about it themselves. On a number of occasions I have been inveigled into games in fraternity houses and never have I encountered an undergraduate whose standard of play was higher than that of the less consequential women's card clubs in the remotest places.

While all this intellectual instruction is being imparted, the freshmen are also taught proper subordination to upper classmen. They must shine the latters' shoes, lend them clothes, answer the doorbell, rake the lawn, shovel snow, and, in the rare instances in which they can write grammatical sentences, prepare papers for the members to use in their classes. Failure to perform their duties properly results usually in a paddling with barrel staves. So important does this loom in the organizations that one chapter of my own fraternity holds annually a paddle dance in memory of the punishment undergone by the freshmen, who expect to inflict it with interest on succeeding pledges.

After a period ranging from three to eight months, initiation takes place. As in the rowdier adult fraternal orders, the ceremonies usually embrace a mock initiation, consisting of horseplay, and afterward the formal induction of the neophyte into the society. Fraternities used to emulate the Shriners and hold their mock initiations in the streets of college towns. They dressed some of the freshmen in women's clothes. Others had to impersonate babies. A favorite stunt was to compel the candidate to bend over and roll a peanut with his nose for half a dozen blocks. Behind him marched the brethren with barrel staves ready to swat him or occasionally to turn the privilege over to a coed whose sadistic impulses sought gratification. While all this was going on, the candidate was required to sing lustily:

> "I have no heart, I have no mind,
> I only know I'm sticking up behind."

So popular was this ceremony that it was finally adopted, to my knowledge, as part of the initiation ceremony of a prominent religious society connected with a State university.

Increasingly onerous police regulations and the demands of the more dignified alumni have driven mock initiations indoors. The only outside initiatory activity now permitted by many chapters is the stealing of chickens from farms near-by. Curiously, in the light of

127

American *mores*, this seems to be confined to the white, rather than the Negro, fraternities.

Except that the audience is smaller, however, indoor mock initiations are little changed from the old style *al fresco*. Occasionally a luckless youth is killed in the process. One very prominent fraternity has had two deaths during initiation within my memory.

The actual initiation services are based mostly on the ritual of various Masonic bodies and the service books of the Roman and Anglican Churches. Kappa Sigma, however, is alleged to follow some of the ceremonies used in the Kirjath Senepher, a society existing in the University of Bologna several centuries ago, whose ritual some of the early Kappa Sig youths unearthed. At least one of the predominantly Southern fraternities is said to employ the rigmarole of the original Ku Klux Klan. The fraternities used regularly to steal each other's rituals, but this is no longer considered ethical.

The ceremonies vary greatly in elaborateness, but are alike in imposing blood-curdling oaths and in revealing the grip, the password, and the teaching of the Greek letters in the fraternity name. These stand for Greek words which constitute either the motto or the secret name of the society. They are not very secret, for any student of Greek can easily guess at them. Several national orders chose their names first, selecting Greek letters that they thought sounded pretty, and then got the local professor of ancient languages to supply a motto to fit. Delta Upsilon, which grew out of a college society representing the views of the Anti-Masonic

128

movement of the early nineteenth century, is the only college fraternity which has no so-called "secrets."

Vestments and other accessories are usually employed in initiations, and some of the more ritualistic orders use them in ordinary business meetings. Sometimes the services are recited with much grace, but commonly their conduct compares with the ritual rendition of an exalted ruler of the Elks about as the latter does with High Mass celebrated by a cardinal archbishop.

Once a member of the fraternity, the youth finds the chapter concerned largely with exemplifying the ritual, paying expenses, giving and attending parties, and participating in college politics. In men's colleges, annual parties for which the men invite girls from their home towns are the principal social events. On such occasions placards appear on the doors of the fraternity houses, reading "Guests Within," lest any of the brethren should thoughtlessly stumble into the living-room with his customary language and gestures. For one such party, some years ago, a fraternity chapter of my acquaintance brought in a houseful of *filles de joie*, accompanied by the mistress of the *maison* as chaperon. Today, I believe, the boys consider such a feat rather a work of supererogation.

Moreover, a great many chapters today have local chaperons, or house mothers, who live in the houses and try to inspire the youth to act like their conception of members of the Union Club. Inasmuch as most of these women are the relics of grocers and retired farmers and have the approximate intelligence of manicurists and deans of women, the imitation is dubious.

A day-by-day picture of life as it is lived in fraternity houses appears in the journals of the orders, which are composed largely of optimistic chapter letters and other personal notes. In them occur such charming and informative items as these:

Charlie Hart was recently elected the university's best dressed man.—*The Shield of Phi Kappa Psi.*

The boys are surely living up to the motto: "A Delta U in everything; every Delta U in something."—*The Delta Upsilon Quarterly.*

Turning from sad thoughts of graduation, the *Palm* reporter directs an anticipatory glance toward the calendar, for the spring dance is not far in the future, and should furnish one of the glad remembrances of college life that will long be remembered.—*The Palm of Alpha Tau Omega.*

Bill —— finally made the grade in March last, and was graduated from Washington—after eight long years of struggling for recognition. At present he is breaking all records as a Buick salesman.—*Phi Kappa Sigma News Letter.*

"My husband," she said, "is a Beta, and he told me that, however distantly I chose to treat strangers, whenever any one asked me about that pin, I was to know he was all right and treat him very cordially. We're from Texas, and he'll be back in fifteen minutes. Sit down and talk with me, please, until he comes, and then we'll all go in to dinner!"—*Beta Theta Pi.*

We understand that Pinkerton and Ebbett have been severely reprimanded by the Department of Child Study for climbing on the roofs of neighboring buildings.—*The Carnation* (Delta Sigma Phi).

Our mothers have formed a club to aid in the welfare of the chapter. The club has already purchased a dozen table-

cloths and six dozen napkins for use in the dining-room.—
The Chi Phi Chakett.

The fraternity journals also publish grandiloquent
articles on college problems, but seldom take a pronounced stand. *The Delta Kappa Epsilon Quarterly,*
however, was a militant opponent of prohibition. The
Chi Phi Chakett assails professionalism in athletics
and *The Signet* (Phi Sigma Kappa) is a vigorous
campaigner for high scholarship.

Occasionally some interested alumnus contributes an
enthusiastic personal experience rebounding to the
glory of the fraternity, such as the following letter,
appearing in the *Theta News* (Theta Kappa Nu):

Kokomo, Indiana.

DEAR DAD:

I do not know how to tell the men of Theta Nu what
a great Fraternity it is but Dad I'm going to tell you
how proud I am to wear the four triangles and will you
tell the boys for me?

One of the happiest days of my life came about this
way: I bought a small restaurant here and was getting
along only fairly well. Tonight about seven p.m. I was
sitting inside, a very dejected boy. Only two had been
in for supper. The cook had gone home and I was all
alone in my meditations.

In came a big blond boy and wanted to sell me a box
of Rinso. I couldn't have bought a gold brick set with
diamonds if he had offered it for a dime. He left, but
soon returned for supper. After I had served him I
noticed he had a fraternity badge on his shirt. I looked
closer and there was the *badge of Theta Kappa Nu.*

131

I shot out my paw and in a second we knew we were brothers. We talked, laughed, and talked some more. Boy! it was great, simply great.

Good luck came following that brother right in, for a nearby shop had worked overtime and here they came until I was swamped.

"Take the kitchen and I'll spin the plates," some one ordered. And say, how that boy could sling hash. After the rush was over we talked until way into the night, just visiting about the greatest Fraternity in the whole world, and incidentally he sold me the box of Rinso. The tide turned and from then on my business picked up.

Let me say right now, Dad, that I am mighty proud to be a *Theta Nu* and a brother to such a prince. I have never found one that did not measure up to *Every man a man.* I want to congratulate Pennsylvania Beta on having as a member of their chapter a man like Brother Paul Behrens.

Fraternally,

H. L. FOUCH.
Indiana, Alpha Beta.

The fraternity magazines also devote much space to laudatory accounts of alumni, ranging from Presidents of the United States and authors of popular novels to winners of dancing contests and head stock salesmen for oil companies. Only ten Presidents have been members of any of the now existing fraternities, and among these Psi Upsilon and Alpha Delta Phi have the lead, with Chester A. Arthur and William Howard Taft belonging to the former and the two Roosevelts to the latter, although Theodore Roosevelt also belonged to Delta Kappa Epsilon. James K. Polk

132

was a member of Kappa Alpha (not connected with either present society of that name), which was founded in 1812 and passed out of existence in 1866. Jefferson Davis, President of the Confederacy, became a member of Kappa Sigma after his retirement from office.

College students, ultra-conservative and full of inferiority feelings, attach great importance to the age of the societies and the difficulty supposed to attend the granting of charters. The oldest of the existing fraternities, Kappa Alpha (Northern), Sigma Phi, and Delta Phi, have together only twenty-one chapters, mostly in small Eastern colleges. These societies are more than a century old. Then there is a larger group of conservative orders, all founded before 1850. Several of these insist that a local organization petition for from ten to twenty years before receiving a charter. In actual practice, the regulation is honored like most college rules. Some years ago, the president of a large Western university, who belonged to one of these ultra-conservative societies, went to the convention and suggested that a chapter be put into his institution. Enchanted by the prospect of Prexy as leading local alumnus, the convention leaped for the bait and installed the chapter within six months.

Other of these societies do what they call "colonizing." This means sending to a college three or four brothers who enrol as students and select other boys whom they like. This scheme originated years ago in the fact that in many colleges each fraternity has a representative on certain class committees. Not infrequently, all the members of a chapter who belonged to a certain class flunked out and were ineligible, where-upon a chapter near by sent at least one man to enroll and represent the lodge on the committee.

In the years following 1850 a number of fraternities were founded, chiefly in the South and the Middle West. Then there was a lull for a time. After 1900, as college enrolments began to grow rapidly, more organizations were established. Most of the existing fraternities also greatly increased the number of their chapters. Today eighty general fraternities exist, with approximately six thousand chapters and a total mem-bership—including living and dead, who for some rea-son are not separated in the statistics—of more than 800,000. They claim ownership of property—most of it mortgaged, however—worth $75,000,000. A few, such as Chi Phi, are heavily endowed. Several fraterni-ties have more than a hundred chapters each. A chapter is not ordinarily required to accept a member of the fraternity who transfers from another college. In some of the older and smaller fraternities, however, there would be a great row if a chapter would actually fail to do this. On the other hand, some of the larger orders very seldom affiliate a man from another chapter, and their conventions, with members of widely different points of view, are as acrimonious as gatherings of Southern Methodists.

In the larger universities, where fewer than half the men, and sometimes only a quarter of them, belong to fraternities, the differences between the chapters seem to the onlooker very slight. This is further borne out by the fact that one man will be rushed by a dozen

134

or more fraternities. In the small New England and New York colleges, where from 75 to 90 per cent of the students are fraternity men, a chapter tends to represent a greater homogeneity, one standing mainly for athletics, another for scholarship, a third for literary pursuits, a fourth for liquor. This tendency, which really was the motivating force in the formation of the early organizations, will, fortunately, grow more marked as larger and larger proportions of men in the colleges and universities join fraternities. There simply won't be enough rich boys or sons of alumni to go around.

A few of the older institutions, such as Princeton, prohibit fraternities, and some others, such as Harvard, give them no encouragement. Some denominational colleges bar them. So do most of the new experimental institutions, such as Reed and Antioch. The rest of the colleges and universities admit them gladly, indifferently, or with thinly veiled hostility. No state now forbids them in its institutions, though anti-fraternity laws in Mississippi and South Carolina were only lately repealed.

This story, like the old barroom ballad, has no moral. The preachers and sewing circles that inveigh against college fraternities might as appropriately attack Rotary International or the Tall Cedars of Lebanon. Likewise, the enthusiastic boys who think their societies are doing noble work for education may be put down as suffering from wish-fantasies. A fraternity may harm an exceptionally talented boy by standardizing him—but so may a college. The society may help

135

a boy who is stupid or seclusive. For the rest, there is little effect one way or the other.

I have met thousands of college students. Unfortunately for my respect for American education, they are pretty much alike. Fraternity men tend to be a little less intellectual and a little more agreeable than the rest. The same thing might be said of the Kiwanians or the Knights Templar.

PROFESSORS OF ENGLISH

IN THE DISTANT PAST, when I still clung to the illusion
that university professors are employed because of,
rather than in spite of, their ability, I heard that
James Lane Allen was receptive to election to the chair
of English in an institution in which he had taken a
great deal of interest. I was much surprised to learn,
subsequently, that the president and board of trustees
had chosen instead a gentleman with Middle English
as his chief concern and a predilection for beginning at least every other sentence with "It is believed
that . . ."

Even in those unsophisticated days I did not consider Mr. Allen one of God's great geniuses, but I had
a suspicion that the author of *A Kentucky Cardinal*
and *The Reign of Law* could, for all his somewhat femi-
nine enthusiasms, do a bit more toward teaching students to write and stimulating their desire to do so,
than could a bespectacled old dodo with his intermi-
nable argument as to how Chaucer actually pronounced
ai and his perpetual fondness for the passive voice even
in conversation. At least, Mr. Allen could sell his work
and people would read it, while the man elected in his
stead could not even give his writings away to the philological journals with their 500–1,000 circulations.

Some ten years ago, an acquaintance of mine, a distinguished scholar and former magazine editor, now in

137

the book-publishing business, was barred from the headship of the English department in a large university for two reasons. In the first place, he had protested years before, in another university, against the antics of a professor of education who wanted to use the English department as "a great and significant laboratory for testing the applications of the principles of educational psychology [whatever that is] to the teaching of the mother tongue of the Anglo-Saxon race." In the second place, he was, so the president of the university told me, a Socialist.

"We can't afford to have radicalism in our institutions of learning, Mr. Crawford," Prexy told me. "How any sane man, with the nation blessed of God with peace and prosperity, Calvin Coolidge in the White House, and almost every workman owning an automobile, can hold radical views, I don't see.

"Your friend Dr. ———— is pleasant to meet and I don't doubt he knows his subject. In fact, I've heard he's a great scholar. But he is boring into our civilization from within." The President lowered his voice, and, leaning toward me shook his finger beneath my eye. "Dr. ————," he went on, "is a Socialist. A Socialist. Think of having a Socialist on a university faculty." The old ignoramus shivered, though it was August.

Dr. ————, I happened to know, was not a Socialist. but a very mild Single Taxer. I did not enlighten the university executive, however. The fear of Socialistic contamination gave him too much fun for me willingly to disturb it. Moreover, I was well aware that distinctions among the various brands of liberal and radical opinion were far beyond the range of his intellect.

Much more recently, the president of a large state university asked me to suggest a man for head of its English department.

"We are going to get the biggest possible man for the place," he declared pompously. "We must have an outstanding writer."

Suspicious though I was, I suggested a poet and a novelist, both of them good scholars, one of them already a university teacher, the other a man who I had reason to know would consider an academic position. They are not, perhaps, outstanding in the world of American letters, but their names would be greeted with respect in any group of critics.

Somewhat later, the name of the appointee to the position was announced. He was the author of two works, one dealing with the Chester mystery plays, the other with the clothes described in Chaucer's *Canterbury Tales*. He had edited several volumes of forgotten authors. He had compiled two anthologies with the Rev. Henry Van Dyke. It was this collaboration, doubtless that ranked him as an outstanding author in the mind of the scholarly Prexy. For in the minds of university presidents, as of deans of women and the suburban clergy, Henry Van Dyke is as great a name in polite letters as Nicholas Murray Butler in education.

Naturally, professors of English thus chosen do not encourage any one to attempt really to teach writing. They themselves do not know how to write—their dissertations are as full of solecisms as a university catalogue is of misinformation—and they have toward the whole writing process a hostility that they can only partly veil. "Research would be Paradise if one did not have to write down one's discoveries in so-called literary form," one of them sadly but frankly remarked to me.

No school of fine arts would let a man teach painting who couldn't paint or a man teach musical composition who couldn't compose. Not only that, but in most institutions he has to produce work from year to year that will stand the test of competent criticism. The professor of painting who did nothing except teach for ten years and then produced a monograph on the probable chemical composition of the pigments used by Domenico Theotocopuli (El Greco) in the winter of 1607-08, would be laughed out of any school of fine arts. Even a university president, brought up on pedagogy and salesmanship, can see that a teacher of painting is supposed to be able to paint, just as the much more important professor of accounting is presumed to be able to make change. But when it comes to writing, the man of learning loses his most previous asset—his nerve—wonders if writing is not after all "a matter of inspiration," and capitulates to the authorities in Gothic, Old English, Middle English, the Minor Poets of the Elizabethan Period, the Restoration Drama, and the Sense of Nature in the Victorian Authors.

A professor of English who has no desire to write and no talent for writing, naturally does not appreciate the technique of the art or the methods by which it can, in some measure, be taught. All that he can grasp is what he calls "gaining facility in our mother tongue" before gatherings of admiring primary school teachers.

Such professors hold the Ph.D. degree in English or Germanic philology, and that seems to them the sole requirement for teaching. Many of them feel that even high school teachers need a knowledge of Gothic, Old English, and Old High German. For instance, Dr. Wilbur E. Gilman of the University of Illinois asserts confidently: "One way of making composition more attractive to immature students is to insist upon a more adequate background in the English language as a requirement for instructors in writing. Although most instructors have had at least one course in Old English and the English Language, their knowledge of the subjects is often somewhat superficial."

Well do I remember a professor of my schooldays who devoted hours to exposition of Grimm's Law and its relation to apparent irregularities in modern English, while most of his students, on the few occasions when they were permitted to recite, said regularly "he done," "has went," and "there ain't but a few." On each occasion, the instructor painstakingly explained the historic origin of the solecism, but without result as to the subsequent practice of the students.

Every now and then, however, through some oversight on the part of the ruling powers, there enters into a department of English a young man of writing ability, who would like to teach his students—or at least some of them—to write. Once the head professors find it out, however, the young man is in for trouble. If he has ever taken any Middle English, they require him to instruct classes in Chaucer. If not, they make him teach composition to great sections of engineers, most of whom are too ignorant to read their own slide rules, let alone peruse a book or write a grammatical paragraph. If against these obstacles he still succeeds in stimulating a student or two to a real interest in writing, the chairman of the department promptly sends for the students and urges them to undertake some work of real importance, such as preparing for research in the mediæval mystery plays or for studying the methods of marking solecisms in freshman English in high school.

When the young instructor is rash enough to write a novel or a series of stories or a few poems, he is promptly advised that promotion or even retention in his job is dependent on "productive scholarship."

"I have no doubt these little things of yours are very interesting," comments the head professor suavely. "Unfortunately, I have not read them. My duties as chairman of the faculty committees on social affairs and women's athletics and my research in the knowledge of Scottish wild flowers possessed by Shakespeare's characters prevent me from reading anything contemporary. But the great writing has been done; nobody can doubt it. A young man of your ability has a great future before him in this institution and in the world of scholarship if he will only devote himself to serious, pressing problems. For instance, I suggest

142

that you undertake the study of the minor English poets of the early fifteenth century. It will open new vistas to you."

Not only among the men does this situation prevail. In my editorial capacity I received recently a story from a young woman who is teaching in a woman's college. "If you print the story," she said, "please use the pseudonym that I have attached. I would be ostracized in my department of English if it should become known that I write short-stories, and, worse yet, publish them." There she put her finger on the essence of the system of values prevailing in typical English departments.

There are, of course, notable exceptions. Henry Seidel Canby still lectures at Yale, though he devotes his major attention to writing. Robert Morss Lovett is at the University of Chicago. Edwin Ford Piper is at Iowa. William Ellery Leonard is on the faculty of the University of Wisconsin. Paul Green is a professor in the University of North Carolina. But Robert Herrick quit the University of Chicago. Percy Marks left Dartmouth. Maxwell Anderson resigned from Stanford. Scores of others have left the teaching of English in disgust and scorn. Some of them would have left anyhow, for any sort of teaching has disadvantages, but not a few would have stayed had the atmosphere not been distinctly hostile. Even those institutions which boast of having a distinguished visiting author "in residence" with a yearly salary on the campus, are careful that he does not occupy too conspicuous a place, and once he begins to show real influence upon

143

the students a flood of resentment arises from the old-time "scholars."

If a university really wants writing taught, there are hundreds of young men now engaged in other tasks —newspaper work, hack writing, clerking—who know how to write and who would jump at the chance to teach it under reasonably congenial surroundings. But the old gentlemen—and ladies—who control the departments of English want not writing ability, but a knowledge of Grimm's Law, an abiding interest in the minor poets of bygone centuries, and, most of all, a proper servility to those in authority. The idea of writing in a university scares them as thoroughly as the odor of incense upsets a Primitive Baptist.

Their opposition to teaching students to write anything that the public will read is manifest in their opposition to the teaching of journalism. For many years in many institutions they successfully fought the introduction of the subject at all. Journalism is, even now, not taught at Yale or Harvard or California, except in the summer session of the last-named institution. The Pulitzer endowment was offered to Harvard and rejected before it went to Columbia. In most of the large institutions, however, the professors of English finally lost their fight, and schools or departments of journalism have been established. In some cases, journalism is a part of the English department, but in most universities the professors of English now have to content themselves with sarcastic comment on the punctuation in the college newspaper and the predilection of that publication for jokes about drinking and necking.

144

Unluckily for my confidence in their judgment, I have read manuscripts by these professors in my editorial labors and found their punctuation even worse than that of the student editors. In certain less formal occupations, I have discovered that they indulge in necking and drinking with a seriousness quite as lamentable as the collegian's ribald spoofing.

Some years ago, I taught English for a short time under a traditional scholar who said to me proudly: "Whenever a student intimates he likes an instructor, I always have him transferred to another teacher. It is a dangerous sign when a boy or girl begins to like a teacher or a study." Most of his fellow-professors today work on the same basis: Make it dull, and it will do 'em good.

In many colleges Genung's works on rhetoric are still the accepted textbooks. These ponderous works, prepared by the Rev. Dr. John Franklin Genung, a Baptist minister long on the faculty at Amherst, are based on the principles and terminology of Latin grammar and Scholastic rhetoric. They abound in definitions of *synecdoche*, *metaphrasis*, *cæsura*, and similar terms. That anybody ever learned from them anything about writing the English language is unbelievable. Their one virtue is dullness.

Those who seek a work more modern but equally virtuous are likely to choose *Freshman English*, a popular textbook prepared by Dr. Karl Young, now professor of English at Yale and his wife, Frances Berkeley Young. The book opens with these illustrious sentences:

"It is now generally agreed that skill in written expression is attained only by practice. In most of our schools and colleges, therefore, students are given a generous amount of the necessary drill through the device of written themes. In order that this drill may be really profitable to the student, he should understand, at the outset, what themes really are, and how he is to go about the writing of them."

Yes, really.

Scattered through the volume are such entertaining, however questionable, statements as, "The longer and more complicated the subject of a theme, the more it needs a formal introduction and conclusion"; and such indubitable discoveries as that "a paragraph must contain neither too much nor too little." Paragraphs, it should be remarked, are divided into those which can stand alone (they "treat the subject completely," the authors say), and those which can't. Of course the authors adopt the orthodox division of writing into exposition, argument, description, and narration, notwithstanding the fact that these are regularly found in as indissoluble union as policemen and whiskey.

Those professors who have developed inferiority feelings about their subject through the jibes of instructors in other studies are likely to turn to *Elements of Literature and Composition,* by the late Dr. Lucius Adelno Sherman of the University of Nebraska. The doctor insists that literature and rhetoric should receive "the same kind of intensive study that chemistry and mathematics have been found to require." When the patronizing chemist or mathematician looks into Dr. Sherman's book, his superior airs promptly disappear. For here are diagrams, charts, and formulæ such as would bewilder the most distinguished physical scientist alive. This, for example, is the analysis of the word "eel":

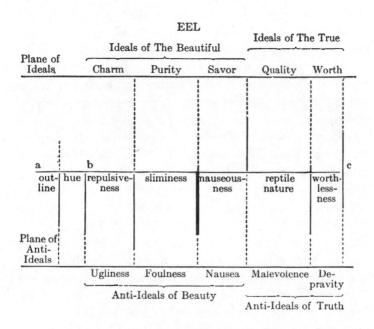

"On mention of the name, if we have ever seen this object, we discern pictorially the 'outline,' and the 'hue,' and draw lines representing these elements towards the lower plane. We draw a line in the same direction for 'elegance' or 'charm,' and also, if we have ever tried to remove an eel from the hook, for the next

147

element. Here the epithet 'slimy,' standing before the
noun of our phrase, administers itself, making us dou-
bly realize that disgusting quality, and shading the
lines drawn to represent it. Then, if we chance at some
time to have eaten fried eels at their best, we draw an
up line for 'flavor,' and a high one. So far we have
recognized 'pleasure' qualities or their opposites. In-
quiring now for Truth elements, we discern little except depraved or 'reptilian' characteristics, and again
draw a downward line, but, on recognizing the place it
fills in the scheme of development, standing between the
genera of serpents and of fishes, we draw a line partly
upward."

Along with such weighty tomes, it is only fair to
state, one finds here and there charming little tricks
and games whereby the student may be persuaded to
learn the peculiarities of his language. One of the most
delightful of these, invented by Professor Theodore
Goodman of the College of the City of New York, is
described at length in the *English Journal* by the
author, who explains that he has used it with marked
success in instructing college seniors. The purpose of
Professor Goodman's device is to teach the difference
between restrictive and non-restrictive clauses, as in the
sentence: "Mont Blanc, which is the highest peak in
the Alps, is capped with snow"; "The boy who wins
shall receive a gold medal."

For the rest, the professor's own scholarly words,
quoted by himself verbatim from his lecture to his
class:

"All toy fire-engines are molded in two longitudinal

148

sections, which are bolted together. In some cases, even the driver is in halves, each part of him being merely a projection of a side of the engine. The result is that we cannot remove him without breaking the toy—ruining it. In other engines, however, the driver is made separately, in a sitting position, with a hook that fits into the seat of the engine. Whether we remove him or not, the engine remains the same.

"The first driver is restricted. He cannot get off. He is part of the toy. Therefore, no hook is needed. The second driver is not restricted. He can stay on, get off, stay off. But as long as he stays on, since he is not a part of the engine, he needs his hook to hold him in place.

"In the sentence, 'The boy who wins shall receive a gold medal,' the clause, 'who wins,' cannot be broken away from the word 'boy' without ruining the meaning. It is not any boy who shall receive a gold medal, but only the *boy who wins*. The clause is restricted; it is molded in one with the thought. We therefore need no hooks.

"In the other sentence, the dependent clause is not really required for the meaning. Other peaks in the Alps, though lower than Mont Blanc, are also capped with snow. One might say that Mont Blanc is capped with snow without making any reference to its altitude. The clause therefore is not restricted; it may remain or go; but as long as it remains, it must be hooked on with commas. For technical convenience, we shall call the first clause *restrictive*, and the second clause *non-restrictive*.

149

"It is often delightful," concludes the great educator, "to play a lesson like a game."

On the other hand, there are those he-men professors who have seen the vision of a vast school of rhetoric, comparable to the school of business administration or even the department of athletics and physical training, in which novelists, poets, short-story writers, essayists, biographers, and journalists could be turned out like marketable wheat from a modern combine.

For example, Duke University, the distinguished Southern Institution which relegated to the rear its dedication to the Blessed Trinity in favor of a cigaret manufacturer who bestowed more appreciation than God Almighty, maintains a course described thus in the university catalogue:

"Students are divided into groups and given assignments in the fields of activity in which they expect to work—such assignments as the presentation of actual business propositions, the exposition of the results of actual scientific experiments, reporting all the many kinds of news in the city and country, the preparation of briefs for law-courts and development of these outlines into finished arguments, the outlining and developing of sermons."

This, of course, is merely the beginning. Duke, not too optimistic, recognizes that there will be numerous young Southern gentlemen who will be satisfied with explaining business propositions, reporting news, and writing sermons. But the others—ah, for them there waits a course called Journalism. This "is planned to satisfy the needs of those who want to become efficient

150

in all the higher forms of writing to be found in newspapers and magazines."

The courses in special kinds of writing usually employ detailed textbooks, full of such original tidbits as the following, from a notable work by Dr. Oscar James Campbell, Jr., of the University of Michigan, and Prof. Richard Ashley Rice of Smith College:

"It is, of course, difficult to be logical."

"To the mere observer life is but a spectacle."

"Every piece of fiction illustrates what the author believes to be some general truth about life."

The development of schools of business, commerce, finance, administration, and their ilk, has of course created an opportunity for teaching "applied English" to their students. The average boy who goes into such schools is as a rule only slightly more literate than the average barber. Much of the work in English, therefore, consists in teaching him to avoid the more egregious errors in grammar when he goes out to sell paint or recommend gaudy but worthless stocks. For the more earnest and intelligent youth, however, there are elaborate drills in "presenting propositions," chiefly oral. The most distinguished authority in this great field is Dr. John Mantle Clapp of New York University, who insists before cheering audiences of business leaders that "communication is essentially an engineering problem—the transportation of an idea from one mind to another." Another analogy by the same authority is this:

"Carrying selling talk to a successful finish resembles the handling of a sail boat. The helmsman watches

151

the water and the wind. He handles his boat so that he will always get the best out of the breeze that is blowing. He may have to tack about a dozen different ways but he always keeps his mind on his course, until he reaches sheltered water, and his boat glides up to her moorings with the tossing sea behind and the cargo safe on board."

To cultivate good vocal habits Dr. Clapp offers many drills in his monumental volume, *Talking Business*. For example, placing the thumb and finger at the corners of the mouth and then repeating:

"We wish we were where Willie went."

Not a few professors of English have adopted charts, graphs, medians, averages, scales of measurement, intelligence tests, and the rest of the paraphernalia of the schools of education, and devote their attention exclusively to teaching their students how to teach English to still other students. There are score cards for textbooks in English. There are tests of sentence recognition, the most elaborate of which was devised by Dr. S. A. Leonard, of the University of Wisconsin, former president of the National Council of Teachers of English. As a matter of fact, all that this test requires is the ability to put periods where they belong. To make it even easier, the inventor explains that a semicolon or even an exclamation point will do instead of a period. One might suppose that after teaching grammar for years, the professors would be ashamed to admit that most pupils can't recognize a sentence lying before them. They evidently are not ashamed, however, for they have collected whole filerooms of statistics on the results and discuss them learnedly in terms of scores, percentiles, median pupils, and total distributions. Dr. Leonard also evolved a series of tests of grammatical correctness. This, as well as the foregoing he dedicated to his State of Wisconsin, so that the systems appear as *The Wisconsin Tests of Sentence Recognition* and *The Wisconsin Tests of Grammatical Correctness.* When, however, he evolved a *Scale of Purely Composition Quality,* he published it with a note, "All rights reserved by S. A. Leonard, University of Wisconsin."

Of course, there are numerous similar scales, though they do not, the professor asserts, accurately measure "purely composition quality," whatever that is. Professor Leonard's principal competitor consists in the Pressey Diagnostic Tests in English Composition. The Hillegas, Minnesota, Harvard - Newton, Nassau County, Lewis, and Willing systems are, however, in common use. Each of them comprises a series of paragraphs that is supposed to represent various stages of attainment for children of various ages.

Some such scales have been put into use even in the colleges and universities. For example, Miss Davida McCaslin, the professor of rhetoric in James Millikin University, has a system whereby every theme handed in is graded as to Thought Value, Structure, Development, and Style.

These would seem glorious foolproof systems, appealing especially to the professor of education, who in the nature of things is none too critical of results. There are, however, surprising mutterings in the edu-

153

cational clan. H. W. James, director of the school of education in Alabama College, intimates strongly that in spite of all the tests and specimens professors of English have no idea how to grade writing. Dr. James got together a group of papers by students, mimeographed them, and sent them to departments of English in all parts of the country. Grades on the papers came back from seventy-five institutions, chiefly very good schools, such as Yale, Michigan, Mount Holyoke, and Wisconsin. On one paper the grades ranged from 20 per cent to 97 per cent; on another, from 40 per cent to 95 per cent; on others there were almost equally wide margins.

An even more fundamental issue is raised, strangely enough, by another professor of education. It is perfectly possible, of course, that professors might not know how to grade a paper accurately and yet be competent and even stimulating classroom teachers. Dr. Franklin Bobbitt, professor of school administration in the University of Chicago, disposed of this matter in a very sour address to a gathering of teachers of English. He declared that "these presented by candidates for the degree of master of arts are marred by an incredible number of blunders in English—sometimes as many as two thousand in a single thesis."

Notwithstanding their contempt for the writing of today—and, for that matter, for all writing—professors of English will journey weary miles to see and hear what the newspapers call "a distinguished author." Their preferences, it is true, are not those of the critics. They would much rather listen to Alfred Noyes than

154

to John Masefield, and they look upon Edwin Markham with much more admiration than upon Robinson Jeffers, Willa Cather, Carl Sandburg, Robert Frost, and Sinclair Lewis combined.

THE AMERICAN ARISTOCRACY

WHEN ALBERT NELSON MARQUIS lost his grand-father, who had brought him up, he was mature enough, at the age of eighteen, to run the old gentleman's store at Hamersville, Ohio, for three years. But general merchandise was no career for a young man who was destined to start a new American enterprise. He went into publishing, eventually reaching Chicago. After fourteen years there, he suddenly broke into the limelight in 1899 with the first volume of *Who's Who in America.*

It was not strictly a new idea; *Who's Who,* the British series, had been running for fifty-one years. But it was new to the United States. True, there were biographical cyclopædias, city, county, and state as well as national, but these were largely rackets. Even where the sketches themselves were not paid for, one might be sure that the banker who was pictured in burnsides and Prince Albert coat and the bishop who appeared in canonical vestments paid a handsome price for the steel engravings.

The good Mr. Marquis had a different idea. A shrewd business man, he felt sure Ben Franklin was right about the dividends of honesty. He put into *Who's Who* the people he thought belonged there and left out the rest. The first volume contained 8,602 names. Every year it has got bigger and bigger, until the 1936–1937 biennial volume includes 31,434 names. The format and binding, which originally followed the British *Who's Who,* have changed only slightly.

Mr. Marquis, who has continued to edit the book, though now with the aid of a staff of assistants, maintains his original policy. Persons holding certain offices get in arbitrarily—high officials of the national and state governments, college presidents, officers of the army above the rank of colonel and of the navy above the rank of captain, bishops, moderators, presidents of ecclesiastical synods. Others are admitted only if the editorial staff thinks they are achieving something important in "a reputable walk of life."

This makes for some curious situations. For example, the bishop of the Pillar of Fire Church (national membership, 2,442)—a lady, by the way, named Dr. Alma White, author of *Why I Do Not Eat Meat* and *The Ku Klux Klan in Prophecy*—is in the book, while the rector of St. Mary the Virgin's, New York City, who probably has ten times the influence and public recognition, is left out.

The book has always shown a strong predilection for the so-called intellectual professions. Considering their number, educators, clergymen, editors, and writers constitute a heavy proportion of the honored ones. Business men are included, but they have to be pretty conspicuous to get in. From the small city in which I live fifty-nine names are listed, but only seven are business men, and four of those are bankers.

While the editors of the book have a deep respect for authorship, their discrimination among writers is curious indeed. For instance, they admit Allen A. Green, author of *The Good Fairies and the Bunnies*, but not T. Swann Harding; Nellie Burget Miller, poet laureate of Colorado by appointment of the governor, but not George Milburn. Among painters one looks in vain for Georgia O'Keeffe and Charles Burchfield, but the book is filled with the names of such second-raters as Clyde Osmer De Land and Elsa Koenig Nitzche.

Gentlemen—and ladies—of the radical persuasion have even harder sledding than the run of modern writers and painters. Max Eastman, gentleman-born, member of the most fashionable and wealthy of all college fraternities, remained in the book so long as he was considered merely a dilettante radical with a charming platform manner. When, however, he began opposing Mr. Wilson's Holy War, he was summarily kicked out. Lately, the war having become an unhappy memory even to self-styled patriots, and Dr. Trotsky having begun contributing to the *Saturday Evening Post* and *Liberty*, the Communistic Mr. Eastman is back among the notables, still proud of his affiliation with Delta Psi.

Michael Gold, at least as distinguished a writer, never was admitted to the sacred portals. Neither was Jack Conroy. Nor was Harbor Allen. And Roger N. Baldwin, the fighter for civil liberties, remains outside. So does William Z. Foster, although he has raised enough hell to be an object of interest to almost anybody. The achievements of radicals are evidently not "useful and reputable" in the minds of the editors.

Nor, for that matter, are those of dancers. A few,

such as Ruth St. Denis and Ted Shawn, are included, but the policy of the editors is against the terpsichorean profession. Indeed, so they told me several years ago when I suggested the name of a well-known dancer as worthy.

On the whole, however, the selections of names in *Who's Who* probably approximates popular judgment. In witness whereof, observe that in the New York *Post's* voting contest for the greatest bore in the city, the leaders in the voting are, with one exception, all included in the book of Great Americans.

When the editors have decided to admit an individual to the company of distinguished Americans, they send him a blank for autobiographical details. The extent to which it is filled is a matter of personal preference. A very few give nothing but their title and address; *e.g.*, George L. and John A. Hartford, respectively chairman of the board and president of the Great Atlantic and Pacific Tea Company. But most notables are not so humble, otherwise they never would have achieved fame. Nicholas Murray Butler has an entire column of biography—approximately three times the space devoted to the President of the United States— while Dr. John Huston Finley devotes thirty-nine lines to listing his organizations and decorations alone, ranging from the Lithuanian Knight of Gediminas to honorary vice-president of the Boy Scouts of Scotland.

An overwhelming majority of the women follow time-honored tradition and omit the date of their birth. Nearly all the men give this item, although a few are kittenish enough not to, among them the editor of the

book, Dr. Marquis. Of each sex there are those who
offer kaleidoscopic variation in their birth dates from
volume to volume. When Andrew Mellon first appeared
in the 1918–19 volume, he was born in 1852. By
1926–27 the date had leaped up to 1854. Since 1930–
31 he has given his birth date as March 24, 1855.

Julia Sanderson, the actress and singer, who entered
Who's Who the same year as the great Secretary of
the Treasury, then said she was born August 20, 1887.
In 1922–23, she wrote the date as August 20, 18... In
1926–27 the date was August 20, 1884. In the most
recent book, she has returned to 1887, but the date is
August 22, a net loss of two days in fourteen years.

The American *Who's Who* omits one item which
adds immeasurably to the entertaining quality of the
British book. That is the heading in each sketch,
"Recreations." Under this title the autobiographer
has scope for his egotism, his humor, his mysticism.
Many of the Britishers merely put down "golf." But
Ezra Pound can write, "the public taste"; Evelyn Un-
derhill, "reading, walking, and talking to cats";
E. Powys Mathers, the cryptic "Three things garnish
our way."

An American with sufficient nerve, it is true, stands
a fair show of getting something of the same sort into
his sketch, notwithstanding the editors' discourage-
ment. For instance, E. Mont Reily, who claims to
have originated the movements that led to the election
of Presidents Theodore Roosevelt and Harding, makes
this boast: "Received letter from President Harding
saying: 'I am now writing you to say that I endorse

160

your entire course in Porto Rico and that your heart has every support from me it can crave.' " Returning to his brokerage business, Mr. Reily reciprocated handsomely with his laudatory volume, *The Truth About President Harding*.

Robert Cameron Beadle, as enthusiastic a Democrat as Mr. Reily is a Republican, brags that he "planned and put in motion the demonstration at Baltimore that resulted in nomination of Woodrow Wilson."

Alice L. Bartlett entertains herself—and the American public—by organizing contests for "best poems on illusion, best poems about science, best poems about animal pets, best poems on the ideal of service, best poems on civilization, best poems on leaders, best poems of flight, best poems on art, best poems packed with thought, best poems about cathedrals, and the best poems about power."

Indeed, *Who's Who in America* is full of quaint information which the subjects of the sketches consider significant. Without this book, most of us would never know—

That Senator Frazier of North Dakota has twins named Unie Mae and Versie Fae.

That Harriet Chalmers Adems captured eight solenodon in Haiti.

That the Hon. James G. Strong enforced prohibition when he was an assistant attorney-general in Kansas.

That Harold Pitcairn, the autogyro and plate-glass magnate, belongs to the General Church of the New Jerusalem, which maintains that the theological writing of Emanuel Swedenborg are "divinely inspired and thus the very word of the Lord."

That John Clayton Allen forty-four years ago got John J. Pershing appointed a military instructor at the University of Nebraska.

That the Rev. James B. Cranfill is not only the editor of *We Would See Jesus,* but the author of *Dr. J. B. Cranfill's Joke Book.*

That Prof. George M. Savage, of Union University, Jackson, Tenn., has read the Greek New Testament through fifty-five times and the Hebrew Bible twice.

That Frederick R. Burnham killed the Matabele god in South Africa.

That Frank B. Linderman, the author, used to be a trapper, a cowboy, an assayer, a newspaper man, and an insurance agent.

That Lewis Nixon, the shipbuilder, has been received in private audience by three kings, two popes, six presidents, and one dictator.

If a distinguished American gets convicted of a notable crime, Mr. Marquis promptly boots him out of the book, leaving only a curt note, *See Vol.* ... This happened to Thomas W. Miller, Albert B. Fall, and even Gene Debs, though the first of these was lately reinstated. A jail sentence doesn't count, however; the noted American leader, Harry F. Sinclair, still holds his place in the sacred volume. If a man is acquitted in court, he has the privilege of bragging about it if he wants to, although few do. The most conspicuous example is Harry Micajah Daugherty, who, just before mentioning his Methodist religion, puts down: "acquitted of charges of conspiracy to defraud the U. S. Govt., 1927."

The pedagogues, always hot for what they call research, have for years studied *Who's Who in America* assiduously, chiefly in an endeavor to prove that one's chances of achieving eminence are vastly increased if one will go to high school and college and listen to the educators. The argument is based on the fact that 85 per cent of the distinguished folk in the book went to college and more than 90 per cent to high school. The fallacy is obvious.

Lately the eugenists have been studying the book, which has given them additional data for their favorite sport of viewing with alarm. It seems notables don't have as many children as the eugenists think they ought to have. Likewise students of the varieties of American religion have examined *Who's Who*, but the intricacies of their argument demand not only knowledge of the Holy Scriptures and the Fathers but divine grace if one is to make head or tail of their views.

Personally I shall not be content until some American scholar deduces from the book what genes and environment are necessary to produce the creator of the civic club musical masterpiece, "Ham and Eggs," and the moderator of the Old Two-Seed-in-the-Spirit Predestinarian Baptist Church.

CATS HOLY AND PROFANE

A PERSON INDIFFERENT TO CATS is as remarkable as a tolerant fundamentalist. As far back as history goes, the cat has been an emotional symbol for both nations and individuals; it has been loved and revered as an incarnation of divinity, or hated and feared as an agent of the powers of evil—and sometimes, with curious ambivalence, it has typified both God and Satan.

In Egypt, as is well known, the cat was sacred to Basta, or Bubastis, the Egyptian Diana, and was, indeed, considered by most of the populace to be the goddess's incarnation. The genesis of the consecration, apparently, was this. Egypt was then, as now, a grain-growing country afflicted with rodents and reptiles. The small Libyan wild cat was domesticated in order to keep down these destructive pests. Undoubtedly it had been the totem of prehistoric tribes or families in Egypt, but now, further to insure its protection, it was made universally sacred by the priesthood of the day. In time, the cat cult attained vast popularity. Although officially only a part of the nation's religion, it became so emphasized that even accidental killing of a cat was the Egyptian equivalent of mortal sin. That thriller of English and American childhood, Henty's *The Cat of Bubastes*, does not depart materially from fact in presenting the feline cultus. Cats that died were mummified, some of them elaborately and at enormous expense, and wealthy families that adhered to the cult often had their mummified cats carried across the country with ceremony and mourning, to rest near the temple of Basta. Today cats are not objects of worship in Egypt, but it is regarded as bad luck to kill, injure, or neglect them.

In Siam the cat does not have the sacredness of the white elephant, but the Royal Cat of Siam (commonly though erroneously called in the United States simply "the Siamese Cat") does possess a certain ecclesiastical quality. The King of Siam does not have to love cats any more than the President of the United States has to love God, but His Majesty, if he is wise and would avoid revolution, keeps a family of the Royal Cats and shows them due respect, just as a President, with his eye fixed on the next election, attends the services of a Protestant church even though his mind during the prayers may be on the candidates for the postmastership at Skaneateles. The populace of Siam would overthrow a ruler who hated cats and admitted it. Even the exportation of Royal Cats from Siam is a difficult business, accomplished only by a bishop, a consul-general, or some one of equal dignity and plausibility.

To take a Manx cat out of the Isle of Man requires almost equal finesse, for there have been numerous movements to pass an absolute embargo act. Here the motive is patriotic rather than religious—though it would have been considered religious not too long ago; the politicians offer the inspiring slogan, "Manx Cats for Manxmen." The Manx cats are presumably the

165

descendants of Oriental, probably Japanese, cats, which came ashore when the Spanish Armada was wrecked. The staunchly Protestant Manx women who converted and married the owners of the cats, likewise led the cats to abjure the errors of both the Pope and the Lord Buddha, and today an Anglican rector on the island without a Manx cat would seem as scandalous as if he lacked a copy of the Book of Common Prayer.

To the Mohammedans a cat is not sacred, but is ceremonially "clean," as a dog is ceremonially "unclean." A sound Moslem will not touch a dog with the tip of his finger, but he will permit a cat to share his plate at dinner and few Mohammedan families are without cats. The uncleanness of the dog is doubtless merely a part of Semitic tradition; the ancient Jews placed dogs with idolaters, sorcerers, and other breakers of ceremonial law. The Hebrew word for *dog* was employed as a euphemism for "male prostitute." Mohammedan friendship for the cat goes back direct to Mohammed himself, who was so fond of cats that he is asserted to have cut a sleeve from an expensive robe on which a cat was sleeping, in order that he might take the robe without disturbing the animal.

The Jews, with their prohibition against images, naturally had no animal totems in historic times. They must have had such, however, before the dawn of history. Indeed, in the Old Testament period, they were inclined to resort to the serpent, the calf, the Phœnician bull of Moloch, and other totemistic symbols of neighboring tribes. The Hebrew Scriptures make frequent reference to animals, but the single reference to

166

cats occurs in the Epistle of Jeremy, affixed in the King James Version to the Book of Baruch, and this was probably written in Egypt. Yet it is hardly credible that cats were unknown to the Jews. If one accepts the purported history in the Book of Exodus, the Jews lived for generations in a country in which cats were omnipresent and sacred. If, on the other hand, one holds, as do most secular historians, that Palestine was even then the home of the Jews but was under Egyptian vassalage, there must have been some governors and tax-collectors religious enough to bring their cats to Palestine with them. Moreover, the Phœnicians, neighbors of the Jews, constantly carried cats from Egypt by ship and introduced the animals even into Italy centuries before Christ. The obvious conclusion is that the Jews knew cats but hated them as the familiars and sacred animals of traditional oppressors. At the same time, from what we know of the Jews' tendency toward the more spectacular religious ceremonies of their neighbors, one may easily believe that there were those who looked wistfully at the Egyptian worship of Basta. It is precisely such ambivalence that would develop a tabu against mentioning the cat. For that matter, famous cat-lovers of mediæval and modern times have all been Gentiles.

There is no mention of cats in the New Testament. They are not known to have been used by the early Christians as ritual symbols, like the fish or the pelican. It is a curious fact that the crocodile was chosen to represent the *Logos*, because of the legend that this animal, like the word, was conceived through the ear

167

and expressed through the mouth. Much more wide-spread, however, was the belief that the cat conceives and gives birth in this way; it was given wide circulation through Plutarch's *De Iside et Osiride.* Yet the early fathers passed over the cat in favor of the crocodile; the influence of tabu seems highly probable.

In Christian hagiography, St. Ives and St. Gertrude became the patrons of cats. These, however, were minor saints, with few rabble-rousing characteristics, and in the Middle Ages the general run of Christians was firmly persuaded that Satan had marked cats for his own.

The priests had convinced them that the gods of the pagan religions, from which they had been converted, were actually devils. At the same time, there remained numerous folk, some of them priests of the older religion, others simple laymen dwelling mostly in remote places, who clung secretly to the ancient faith. In their ceremonies, held in secret far from the eyes of the pious emissaries of Rome, cats not improbably figured; and certainly it was common Christian belief that they did so figure.

The mediæval Church was as full of the lore of demons as of the miracles of saints. Every Christian peasant and every pious priest—unless he were definitely of the Schools—felt infinitely more sanguine of encountering a witch than an archangel along the king's highway. The Devil was ever watchful over his own and saw to it that at least one competent witch was provided for every parish. The universal belief in witchcraft, the traditional association of cats with the old pagan religion, rumors of the clandestine doings of still remaining devotees of the ancient faith—all tended to place the cat, especially the black cat, as an emissary or even an incarnation of Satan. The sparks from static electricity generated when a cat is stroked added conviction to the belief. Further, the mediæval Catholic, like the modern Baptist, was heartened in his faith by a clergyman who slapped him on the back in good-fellowship. That was religion worth while. The cool aloofness of a dignified cat was disconcerting and vaguely alarming. The result was that innumerable cats suffered unspeakable torments in the progress of Christianity among the morons. Coupled with the Christian superstitions of the people was the fact that the Druidic religions had enjoined sacrifice of animals, apparently to insure plant and animal fertility. Thus the members of a mediæval parish, when they burned cats alive, were fulfilling the demands of their ancient creed—which lingered in their minds— and at the same time were destroying the incarnation of the old-time gods considered as devils. The act represented the ambivalence characteristic of all popular religious experience down to the contemporary disciples of Buchman, who obtain the erotic thrills forbidden by St. James while they engage in the confessions which he commanded.

From these cruel antics of the common people, the most intelligent of the clergy held aloof. Many of them, including a number of popes and cardinals, were devoted to cats. The monks of Chartres invariably raised blue cats in their monasteries, undeterred by the fact

169

that black cats often appear in litters from blue parents. Undoubtedly such clergy were not unmindful of the symbolism of the cat as the *Logos;* assuredly they must have found a cat both more Christianly charming and more practical than a pet crocodile.

This symbolism, mixed with a popular dualism, led to a strange annual ceremony at Aix, in Provence, if descriptions of it may be believed. Each year the largest and handsomest male cat that could be obtained was exposed to the gaze of the faithful on the festival of Corpus Christi. On St. John's Day, shortly after, a group of cats was burned alive with equal ceremony. The burning of cats on St. John's Day was not confined to Aix, but was common to numerous places, a probable relic of the Druidic summer festival. The ceremonies at Aix, however, suggest something even more primitive; the worship of a deity and his sacrifice shortly thereafter. These ceremonies, moreover, are evidence not only of the antiquity of the average person's religious notions, but of his unshakable belief in both God and the Devil and his inability to distinguish between the two. The common man, in mediæval France as in modern America, has no love for God; his sole religious ideal is to compel or wheedle the divinity and thus escape being persecuted by the secular arm on earth and pitched into liquid fire, to the accompaniment of a sermon by St. Dominic or John Calvin, in the hereafter.

The mediæval ecclesiastical courts heard ample evidence of the devilish propensities of cats as familiars of witches or incarnations of Satan himself. Cats turned beer sour, wrecked ships, produced disease, led armies, desecrated crucifixes. One theologian maintained that every cat served seven masters, each for seven years, and then carried the soul of the last into hell. The Protestant reformers held these beliefs with equal fervor, along with such variants as that the pope traveled in the form of a black cat to confound honest Christians.

Many superstitions about cats prevalent today are traceable immediately to concepts of witchcraft. The most common is the superstition about a black cat's crossing one's path and thus marking one's way with the sign of Satan, although probably few residents of the United States would think of sprinkling holy water, making the sign of the cross, or beginning the formulary, *Te exorciso*. They might, of course, touch wood, which any theologian could tell them brings the virtues of the True Cross into play against the wiles of the adversary.

Almost equally common is the belief that a cat will suck a baby's breath or steal his blood. Obviously, the cat is an incubus wreaking his vile intentions on the infant, or is the Devil himself, who wants the blood of the child to use in the Black Mass.

I conjecture that the proverb, "A cat may look at a king," goes back much further than these superstitions. The cat was commonly a totem animal. The king, or chief of the tribe, often was tabu to the members of the tribe to such an extent that to look upon the royal face meant death. It was necessary, however, for representatives of the tribe at times to consult the chief face to face. The totem animal possessed this privilege as a matter of course, and what would be more natural than for the tribal representative to impersonate the animal and thus avoid the tabu? Impersonation of totems still exists in some tribes.

In widely separated parts of the world, there were other primitive beliefs about the cat, many of them relating in some way to fertility, and some survive to this day. Frazer refers to the use of the cat in rain-making magic in Celebes and Java. People as distinct as Russian peasants and the primitive Oraons of Bengal believe that people may turn themselves into cats which suck from female animals and murder male animals. In both German and French folklore the beneficent corn-spirit is a cat. In Teutonic mythology the chariot of Freya, goddess of love, was drawn by cats. The striking fact about these instances is that, depending on the regional beliefs, the cat is loved as a bringer of fertility or hated as a destroyer of it.

The average person who dislikes cats may have no conscious superstitions about them, but his dislike is informed with heavy emotional content. He is not content with a Doctor-Fellian attitude—"the reason why, I cannot tell." He offers always numerous reasons for his dislike.

These reasons for disliking cats, of course, are rationalizations, as for that matter are the reasons that I or any other cat-lover gives for liking the animals. From the earliest times the cat has been so invested with emotional import that it cannot be viewed coolly. The cat-hater has developed and maintains his aversion

172

for reasons of which he is unconscious. Actually, one of the leading psychiatrists of the United States assures me, all dislike for cats is essentially fear of cats; that it does not usually develop into the pathological symptoms immediately recognizable as ailurophobia, is due to its not being severe or to its being repressed.

There probably exists no animal for which some persons do not possess a pathological phobia, but fear of cats—ailurophobia in English, *Kazenphobie* in the more accurate German—is widespread and has been for centuries. It appears chiefly in women, although men—witness Napoleon—are also subject to it.

Symptoms range from discomfort in the presence of a cat to outright terror, with chills, hysterical laughing and crying, locking of the jaws open or closed, fainting, convulsions, hallucinations, and even temporary blindness. Persons afflicted with ailurophobia are often able to detect the presence of a cat hidden in a room long before more normal persons know anything about it.

Two explanations for the phobia used commonly to be given. One was that the individual had been frightened by a cat in childhood. The other was that there existed in him a racial memory of the time when mankind was in constant terror of the saber-toothed tiger and other great cats. Both explanations were attacked early in the twentieth century by Dr. S. Weir Mitchell, the novelist and descriptive neurologist, who investigated a large number of cases of cat fear. He found that practically none of the cases studied had any his-

tory of fright from a cat in childhood. This of course
is not conclusive, because one tends to forget unpleasant occurrences, but its evidential value has been rein-
forced by detailed psychiatric studies in more recent
years.

Dr. Mitchell disproved the racial memory theory by
the simple test of having the ailurophobes go to a zoo
and watch the lions, tigers, and leopards. Most of them
were not disturbed in the least; a few, though unaf-
fected by the larger cats, developed hysterical symptoms at sight of small wild cats resembling domestic
cats. In this study also, Dr. Mitchell's conclusion is
confirmed by psychologists and psychiatrists, most of
whom consider that racial memory probably does not
exist.

The learned doctor confessed himself without a theory as to the causes of ailurophobia, except in those few
cases where the emanations from a cat's fur gave rise
to asthmatic symptoms. In the last quarter of a century, however, psychiatric investigation has reached
certain conclusions which have been generally accepted
in modern scientific circles.

According to these views, ailurophobia is simply one
of the phobias that afflict human beings. It is comparable to agoraphobia (fear of open places) and topo-
phobia (fear of moving) but is more common than
these and consequently less likely to be recognized by
the lay observer as clearly neurotic. The physical and
hysterical symptoms tend to be much alike, however,
in all phobias.

Any phobia is the result of emotional conflict between two desires; one of them, commonly, a natural animal desire, the other a moral or religious feeling. The phobia, as Stekel points out, is a compromise in the conflict—a truce, enforced with the aid of anxiety. For this reason modern psychiatry groups all phobias under "anxiety hysteria," the translation of a term first applied by Freud.

It follows that the victim of a phobia does not fear the object *per se;* rather, as a symbol. Also, the individual's feeling toward the thing symbolized is compounded of both love and hate. The object—whether it is, for instance, an open space or a cat—represents something for which the person yearns but which he has relinquished or thinks he has relinquished, usually for purported ethical reasons. The yearning that arises afresh upon sight of the symbol is thwarted, and converted into fear of the symbol.

Now as to fear of cats. The cat is an erotic symbol —to most persons a female symbol, as certain words in English, German, and French slang make clear enough. Among persons of European descent at least, the cat is commonly taken to represent, further, the "evil mother," as opposed to the "good mother,"—the Blessed Virgin Mary, a woman's patron saint, or perhaps her own mother. The evil mother is traditionally a goddess of the pagan religions preceding Christianity; she is a witch who has sold her soul to Satan; she is the "priestess of diabolical succession" who celebrates the Black Mass, or, according to a variant, the devotee on whose naked body the blasphemous sacrament is celebrated. In other words, the cat typifies the specifi-

175

cally sexual character in woman—which, in any Puritan civilization, means evil.

The relatively few persons to whom the cat is a male symbol think of the remarkable potency of male cats and also of the sadistic elements in the cat's character. (Actually, of course, the cat combines masochistic and sadistic components to an extent that should delight any psychoanalyst. The cat is cruel—and urbanely kind; it is aggressive—and passive.)

Some women who fear cats have, so investigation has shown, powerful homosexual desires that have been kept below the level of consciousness by the pressure of conscience. Such a woman fears the cat, the female symbol, which typically represents the first woman to whom she was strongly attracted; all women (since they are possible objects of sin); and the part of her own character which tends toward inversion.

Most cases of cat phobia are not so simple as the one which I just related. Notwithstanding the efforts of Dr. Jung and his disciples, the study of the human mind cannot be reduced to formularies. A psychoanalyst who has analyzed numerous children tells me that cats appear frequently in their dreams and are evidently sexual symbols but of varied significance.

In many, probably most, cases of adult ailurophobia, the basis is exceedingly complex. For example, a woman described by Stekel associated cats with crocodiles (the two animals symbolizing the *Logos*), and with clergymen (this perhaps being associated with marriage, perhaps with the idea of the *Logos*, ostensibly, however, with a story remembered by her). She told Dr. Stekel that even the words *Geistlicher* and *Vikar* aroused the cat-fear in her. In childhood she had a dislike for furs and an actual fear of her father's traveling coat, which seemed to her made from a number of cats.

The woman was by no means the typical neurotic. The wife of a physician, she carried on important scientific work of her own. But fear of cats, accompanied by passionate love for dogs, she admitted, determined much of her life. The only cat that she was ever able to view without dread was one which wore a bell around its neck and made its bed with a dog.

She attempted psychoanalysis and other forms of psychiatric treatment for her phobia, but with little success. A psychoanalyst—not Dr. Stekel—traced her fear to a passion for a governess.

Stekel, on the other hand, tentatively attributes the phobia to excessive love for her father and jealousy of her brothers and sisters.

"The patient sees in the cat the mirrored image of herself," he explains. "She is the false cat that with boundless jealousy envied her brothers and sisters the parents' love. She saw incorporated in the cat the criminal ideas of her childhood. Her wild impulses manifested themselves early, but soon there developed a sensitive conscience which suppressed everything bad and projected it outward upon the cat. She suppressed, too, all sexual emotions, so that she was able to enter unenlightened into marriage and to believe in conceiving through a kiss. . . .

"The cat is the tyrant of her existence, the representative of the false. The dog, the symbol of the true, is her friend. In her soul dog and cat wage an embittered strife. She could bear the sight of but one cat. That was the kitten with the bell, which lived happily with the dog. The cat's bell may have reminded her of her conscience, which continually sounds the warning, 'Be on guard against yourself.' "

A case discussed by Dr. Helene Deutsch in the *Almanach der Psychoanalyse* for 1931 is equally complex. Here the patient, likewise a woman engaged in scientific pursuits, had been in love with both men and women, and had been masochistic and exhibitionistic. She had a phobia not only for cats but also for heights —as mountains—and for the sea.

Dr. Deutsch traced the fear of cats to jealousy of her mother, for whose death she wished in childhood. She overcompensated for this by an apparent overwhelming love for her mother. Her relations with other women were motivated by aggression against women (typifying her mother), which was transformed, however, into apparent passivity and love. In her unconscious existed both a sense of guilt and a fear of the death that she had desired for her parent.

The *Katzenphobie* had the folklore fantasy back of it. The cat symbolized to the patient the witch, the counterpart of the good fairy. The fear that she felt was directed toward the great danger—presumably death itself—that seemed to threaten her through the witch, the wicked woman, in her own conscience.

In folklore the cat appears occasionally not as a witch but as, in a restricted sense, the good fairy; for

178

example, the stories of Puss in Boots and of Dick Whittington and his Cat. In these and similar tales the cat procures a fortune for its master. Genetically, such legends go back much further than does the witch concept; they represent the cat as a fertility symbol. Where this concept of the cat appears in connection with a phobia, it is considered to carry an anal-erotic connotation, by reason of its association with the collection of money.

The somewhat rare man who has a pathological fear of cats is interpreted differently from the woman ailurophobe. His phobia may represent an unconscious distaste for women, as symbolized by cats. Or it may stand for a fear of the aggressive sexual components of his own character, in which instance he regularly thinks of the cat as male, not female. I have often encountered the latter peculiarity among men who are not wholly upset by the sight of a cat but who have a highly emotional dislike for cats.

Fear of cats or antipathy for them thus is always symbolic, associated with persons, with feared or disliked traits in the individual's own character, and often with folklore and tradition. A similar statement may be made about us who (perhaps even to a pathological degree) love cats. We identify them with persons whom in childhood we admired, and we see in them our own best qualities or the qualities which are not ours but which we should like to possess. Just as tribes or families in the early days of the human race adopted animal totems not only as their own protectors but as their ostensible ancestors, so the child, recapitulating

179

the history of the human mind, chooses his animal totem, and the cat is a common selection. The choice may be due to a variety of unconscious factors. The cat may be a female symbol, the embodiment not of the witch, however, but of the good, the desired mother. On the other hand, there may be admiration of the traditional sexual powers of the cat (usually a father identification on the part of the child). Again, the cat may stand for the perfect freedom longed for by the overprotected or repressed child. A more bizarre case is found when the son or daughter of a preacher, revolting against the theology of the father, does not become a bank robber or a prostitute—as the godly expect from such heresy—but symbolizes the revolt by special affection for the cat, representative of traditional opposition to Christianity.

My own fondness for cats goes back, I believe, to the fact that in childhood I was disturbed by those who over-emotionalized everything, notably the trivial. Instead of accepting their point of view, I revolted against it, and the cat, cool, detached, unsentimental, became a symbol of the qualities that I admired. This diagnosis, I admit, is superficial—no one can psychoanalyze himself—and there doubtless are much deeper reasons for my interest in cats.

In nearly all lovers of cats I find a certain contempt for the stupidity of mankind. The famous cat-lovers of history—Petrarch, Isaac Newton, Wolsey, Richelieu, Dr. Johnson, Baudelaire, Gautier, Anatole France, Swinburne, Wordsworth, Poe, Mark Twain, Whittier, Longfellow, Ellen Terry,—have had little in common save realization of the low intellectual and ethical estate of humanity. Whittier and Longfellow may seem at first blush to be exceptions. Longfellow, however, got so bored with his stupid students at Harvard that he resigned his professorship. If Whittier was too gentle to express his contempts in words, perhaps even to recognize them consciously, he symbolized them by an ascetic life largely removed from human contacts.

Rightly or wrongly, the cat to many intellectual persons, especially writers, typifies the godlike wisdom to which man pretends but which he never attains. To them the cat is essentially a god. Not, of course, a popular American god, watching over the grain market on week days and over the First Methodist Church on Sunday morning. Rather, a tranquil, meditative, elegant, graceful god. "I have studied many philosophers and several cats," Taine remarked. "The wisdom of the cats is vastly superior."

Any one who holds this point of view is undisturbed by the fact that cats do not fawn. He has no illusion that any god is going to reward him by visible sign of divine favor. He does not even expect his pastor as God's vicegerent to slap him on the back and predict that his golf game will improve because he voted against that infamous wet Catholic who ran for county clerk.

Naturally, the typical American, with his tremendous inferiority complex and his consequent tremendous need for external praise, has little admiration for cats. Even if he had no childhood associations to contend with, the coolness of the cat would convince him either that the animal was too unintelligent to recognize his greatness or that, recognizing it, the cat deliberately and deceitfully disregarded it. On the other hand, the dog appeals perfectly to his inferiority feelings. It fawns upon him and makes extravagant demonstrations over him, giving him daily a thrill comparable to that which comes from the annual Rotary award for perfect attendance. The dog, I am convinced, was really the first Rotarian. When a dog leaps upon me with barkings and tail-waggings, I always half expect him to slap me on the back, call me by my first name, and invite me to join him in singing "Ham and Eggs."

Not a few persons identify themselves with dogs— the result of childhood experiences. Indeed, I am inclined to think that every first-class salesman or contact man has adopted this identification. College cheer leaders, officers of the D. A. R., and peripatetic evangelists belong in the same category.

To dogs, however, much more indifference exists than to cats. Pathological fear of dogs, while known, is rare. Nor have dogs often appeared as sacred symbols.

The genesis of the stronger emotional values attached to cats is lost in the unwritten history of the evolving human mind. One may make certain conjectures, however. Physical characteristics of the cat, such as its changing eyes and the static electricity in its fur, doubtless gave it an atmosphere of mystery. Moreover, the cat has a peculiar intelligence or insight, so different from that of man that it must have attracted notice very early. A common act of cats—to approach with friendly purrs one who fears them—is sometimes cited by the thoughtless as an indication of lack of intelligence, but is recognized by animal psychologists as precisely the opposite. A phobia is always ambivalent, representing love as well as hate, and the cat recognizes the love repressed beneath the cloak of fear. Such insight is considered by spiritists, theosophists, and other spook-chasers a sign of occult power. In animistic and immediately following times, this belief must have been universal. Subsequently, the cat prospered or suffered in accordance with the vagaries of racial religion and thought.